Alua Dumysheva

The ideology of tennoism - imperial power in modern Japan

Alua Dumysheva

The ideology of tennoism - imperial power in modern Japan

ScienciaScripts

Imprint

Cover image: www.ingimage.com

This book is a translation from the original published under ISBN 978-3-659-85179-7.

Publisher:
Sciencia Scripts
is a trademark of
Dodo Books Indian Ocean Ltd. and OmniScriptum S.R.L publishing group

120 High Road, East Finchley, London, N2 9ED, United Kingdom
Str. Armeneasca 28/1, office 1, Chisinau MD-2012, Republic of Moldova, Europe
Printed at: see last page
ISBN: 978-620-8-35001-7

Table of Contents

A word of thanks... 2
Terminology dictionary 3
Introduction 5
Chapter 1: Ideology as the spiritual core of society 11
Chapter 2: Shaping the Political Priorities of Postwar Japan 38
Conclusion 71
LIST OF REFERENCES USED: 76

A word of thanks...

I want to express my gratitude to all those people who helped and supported me in my endeavor. Special thanks to my supervisor, Doctor of Historical Sciences, Professor Anuar Abitaevich Galiev for his incredible support in the process of my research work. Under his strong guidance and professionalism my previous monograph "Image of South Korea and Japan on the territory of the Republic of Kazakhstan: a comparative aspect" was published.

Terminology dictionary

Kokutai (Japanese: 國體?, "Body of the Nation", in modern characters - 国体) is an ideological construct, a set of ideas that make up the national identity of the Japanese. Its origin dates back to the Edo period, when the philosopher Aizawa Seishisai formulated the basic idea of kokutai as some unbreakable ties between the Japanese emperor and his subjects, which ties, according to the philosopher, constituted the "body of the nation". Later, the concept of "kokutai" came to include everything that the Japanese considered to be unique features of their nation, such as religion (Shintoism), state structure, military spirit (bushido), and so on. During the Shōwa period, when the country's far-right militaristic and parafascist forces became more active, kokutai was used as state propaganda that simultaneously asserted the Japanese people's profound differences from all other nations and Japanese superiority over them. After Japan's defeat in World War II, the popularity of kokutai as an instrument of state propaganda declined significantly. *Klaus J. Antoni.* Shinto und die Konzeption des Japanischen Nationalwesens, Kokutai. - BRILL, 1998. - 426 c. - ISBN 9789004103160.

Tenno (Japanese: heavenly sovereign), title of a Japanese emperor. In literature, especially outside Japan, the term mikado is also used. Encyclopedic Dictionary http://www.vedu.ru/bigencdic

Shogun is the title of the rulers of Japan in 1192-1867, under whom the imperial dynasty was deprived of real power. There were three Shogun dynasties in all: Minamoto (1192-1333), Ashikaga [1335(1338)-1573], Tokugawa (1603-1867). Encyclopedic Dictionary http://www.vedu.ru/bigencdic

Shogunate - the government of the Shoguns in Japan from 1192-1867. It was also called bakufu. Encyclopedic Dictionary http://www.vedu.ru/bigencdic

Kojiki - Records of ancient deeds

Amaterasu (Japanese:天照大神 amaterasu o:mikami?, "the great deity who lights up the heavens") is a sun goddess, one of the main deities of the all-Japanese Shinto pantheon, according to Shinto beliefs, the ancestress of the Japanese imperial family. It is believed that the first Emperor Jimmu was her great grandson. Ruler of the Heavenly Fields Takamagahara (Jap. 高天原?). According to legend, in the past Emperor Shōmu had difficulty completing the Great Eastern Temple of Todaiji and the grand statue of Buddha Vairochana there. When he asked Amaterasu for help through the seventh- and eighth-century miracle-worker Gyōchi, the goddess replied that she was the Buddha Vairochana. Nevertheless, this legend probably appeared much later than the events it describes, as the first mentions of it date back to the second half of the 13th century[1]. AMATERASU // Japan from A to Z. Popular illustrated encyclopedia. (CD-ROM). - Moscow: Directmedia Publishing, "Japan Today", 2008. - ISBN 978-5-94865190-3.

Introduction

Relevance of the research topic. The relevance of this work is determined by the fact that the world is increasingly shaken by the tendencies of manifestation of discontent among the population in relation to the economic, social and sometimes cultural policy of the country's management. And as a consequence, these discontents cause irreversible consequences for the state, destabilizing the political, economic and social situation in the country. In this regard, today there is an urgent need to find a way to solve such problems that hinder the further development of the country. And Japan, as a country with a fairly stable political, social and economic system, attracts attention not only by its success in the field of economy, scientific and technological progress, but also by its originality, originality and special spiritual wealth.

Japan is a mono-national state and Japanese nationalism is a special ideological construct, long ago created by the ruling elites in order to meet the internal and external needs of the nation, its specific interests... What is ideology? Ideology is a system of views, ideas that characterize a social group, class, political party, society. The state emerges and preserves its identity, first of all, thanks to the state ideology. The power of the state is strengthened precisely by ideological unity, thoughtfulness of the strategic line. Natural resources, economic opportunities, armed forces, political system - all this can bring greater success and benefit if there is a unified strategic line of the state. It is the state ideology that determines the development strategy. The very formation of the state is unthinkable without the creation of a new ideology corresponding to this state. Only on the basis of the state ideology the unifying role in society can be played by the personality of the leader, the political figure who creates the state, the elite of society.

State ideology is defined as a system of worldview, political, moral, economic, religious values shared, accepted by the majority of society. There is always an internal core that ensures national unity throughout the centuries. State ideology allows to ensure internal stability, cohesion of the people into a single whole to achieve the strategic goals of the state. In addition, the state ideology creates a special spiritual and moral climate in society, influences the consciousness and feelings of people, their behavior, attitude to the authorities, interethnic, inter-confessional relations and relations between social strata. The presence of state ideology in society gives citizens a sense of involvement in the development of the country, regardless of their nationality, religion and social status. In addition, the state ideology should correspond to the mentality of the people, come from the depths of the people, be based on the traditions of spiritual values, principles of life, way of life of the people. As it happens in Japan. The Japanese authorities, activating today the ideologies of Tennoism and state nationalism, "tell" the society from positive positions about the special uniqueness of the Japanese nation, about its huge creative potential, as well as about the tasks of the authorities to preserve and improve it. At the same time, the ruling elite of Japan every time neatly "hints" to the nation that its survival in the hostile world environment in the XXI century is possible only on the way of uniting the collective efforts of all Japanese "under the leadership of the emperor and the state" to protect the independence and sovereignty of the country and fulfill the priority tasks of national development. The structure of such an ideology could become an excellent illustrative example for young, recently independent states. In particular, for Kazakhstan, since our country, like all post-communist countries, has experienced the collapse of ideology and is now intensively searching for a national idea to consolidate the nation. In the search for an idea, they turn to the experience of Western and Eastern countries, and to traditional values. In our opinion, the experience of Japan, and Tennoism in particular, should be studied. It is not a question of adopting Japan's political system in its entirety, even with a great desire, this will not work. It is about the specificity of the life position of this nation. Corporate spirit, the desire to do everything for the good of the country, because the country is the people, that is, they do for the good of themselves, thinking about the future. After all, at first glance it is surprising how such a strong state with such a small territory can keep its industry and economy at the top, and still be able to preserve its national originality, amazing nature, etc. The Japanese are accustomed to use everything rationally, in everything they try to come to the ideal. And the ideology of Tennoism has played a huge role in the Japanese character. We should adopt these humanistic values in our society. After all, with the help of the ideology of Tennoism, the Japanese government manages to maintain stability in the political, economic, social and cultural spheres of the state.

The purpose of this paper is to investigate the ideology of Tennoism, which contributed to the establishment of a stable political system in the country.

In accordance with this goal, the following objectives were set:

1 .Analyze the ideology of Tennoism.

2 .Examine the influence of religion on the formation of ideology.

3 .Examine the ideology of Tennoism as a state national policy.

4 .On the basis of the obtained data, identify the features of the modern political system.

The object and subject of the study.

The object of the study is Japanese society.

The subject of the study is the ideology of Tennoism as a fundamental factor in the formation of the modern political system of Japan.

Methodology. According to modernist theory, it is in the period of modernization that the state and ruling elites mobilize and unite the nation with the help of a new nationalist ideology, usually more aggressive and offensive than the previous one. And this is done in order to fit more easily into the new system of international relations, the stable stay in which, as a rule, is associated with new challenges and threats to the survival of the nation. In defining nationalism in general, Max Weber once correctly, in our opinion, emphasized that nationalism is an ideology created by the authorities for society and offering it its "story" about the "good" nation, its relations with the state and with other countries

Research method. The topic of this study is interdisciplinary in nature and is at the intersection of several sciences: political science, history, psychology, theory of ideology. The interdisciplinary nature of the work predetermined the need to use the basic principles of systemic, institutional and structural-functional approaches in analyzing the ideological elements of political processes. In the thesis work the principles of socio-analytical, cultural-historical and comparative methods of research are mainly applied.

The novelty of the research topic is determined by the fact that it represents the first attempt in domestic science to consider the influence of the ideology of Tennoism on the political system, public consciousness and on the cultural life of the Japanese people.

The source base for this work was the following works: mythological sources on the origin of the imperial house, the constitution of Japan, official documents, electronic and print media (materials of newspaper publications, websites).

The extent to which the topic has been studied.

The topic of this study is multidimensional in nature, which predetermined the need to study and compare extensive material of both normative and doctrinal nature. Scholars of Russia and Central Asia have repeatedly addressed the problems related in one way or another to the institution of imperial power in Japan. T.G. Sila-Novitskaya, in particular, studied the history of the development of the cult of the emperor in Japan and wrote a monograph that traces the history of the cult of the emperor from antiquity to the present day, examines the dogma and evolution of the doctrine of monarchism, and analyzes the cult of the emperor in modern Japan. The book helps to better understand the origins and peculiarities of Japanese nationalism, the mechanism of interaction between official ideology and mass consciousness. Religions also played an important role in the formation of the ideology of the Japanese people, which later influenced the political structure of the country. The Japanese model of religious life in her works studied by E.V. Molodiakova. In her works she states that the formation of the political system of the country was influenced by three major religions: Shintoism, Confucianism and Buddhism.

Our domestic, in particular, Japanese scholars in their works have repeatedly drawn their attention to the structure of the political system and public administration of Japan. N.J. Shaimardanova in her works considers the formation of the political system of Japan from the post-war period to the present day. And since the purpose of the thesis is to study the foreign experience of state formation for recently independent states, such as Kazakhstan, we studied the materials of KISI under the President of the Republic of Kazakhstan, in particular the book "Reforming the system of public administration: foreign experience and Kazakhstan". This book is devoted to topical problems of development of public administration system of Kazakhstan. The book analyzes foreign experience in the functioning of public administration and outlines the main approaches to further reforming of public administration in Kazakhstan. Also were studied and analyzed the works of B.V.Pospelov, who believes that one of the important features of the functioning of the state in Japan is an active ideological activity aimed at preserving the ideological and political basis of the capitalist system.

Despite the abundance of studies devoted to the political process and the influence of ideological factors on it, the modern research literature is dominated, with some modifications, by one approach in interpreting the sources of the political process, which is reduced to understanding the political process as conditioned almost exclusively by objective and primarily economic factors. The limitation of this approach is that it actually ignores the subjective component of politics as an activity not directly related to economic interests and, ultimately, levels the idea of free will in politics. The notions of external "objective" determinacy of political processes are inherently anti-humanistic. In addition, they are unable to adequately explain a number of phenomena of political life in modern society. This includes the ideological and value bases of politics. Modern understanding of the relationship between the political process and ideology implies the need to apply other conceptual schemes to analyze these phenomena.

Chronology of the thesis topic: from the 7th century A.**D**. to the present day

Approbation of the work. This work was approved in the collection of works of students, graduate students and schoolchildren, dedicated to the 20th anniversary of the Republic of Kazakhstan and the 70th anniversary of Abylai Khan KazUMOIMYA "We are patriots of Kazakhstan, let's build the future together" (Almaty, 2012). Also, this work was tested in the student magazine published at the Department of World Cultures and Civilizations of the Faculty of Oriental Studies "Orient.kz".

Structure of the work. The research work consists of an introduction, two chapters, conclusion, appendices and a list of references.

Chapter 1: Ideology as the spiritual core of society

The explanatory dictionary gives the following definition of ideology "...is a system of views, ideas that characterize a social group, class, political party, society."[1, p.236] In principle, from a scientific point of view, the definition is quite accurate. And to the ideological life of Japanese society is quite suitable universal formulation, according to which ideology is "a set of doctrines, theories and assessments relating to the phenomena of social life and given from the position of a certain class, expressing its fundamental interests and goals and strengthening its social position .... With the help of ideology the attitude of people to social reality and each other is evaluated, it reflects social problems and contradictions, as well as programs of activity aimed at preserving and developing or changing existing social relations. Ideology is expressed in the existing legal, political, moral, artistic, religious and economic views " [2, p.28]. Any society has its own system of views, ideas, formed over centuries, passing from generation to generation, which characterizes it as a full-fledged society, which helps to keep up with the times, not losing its identity, uniqueness, not forgetting traditions, customs inherited from ancestors. In the modern world under conditions of globalization, it is difficult to preserve its identity, but, in particular, the Japanese people and nowadays manage to preserve and continue to carry their culture, traditions and customs further in step with the times. Creating something new and being several steps ahead of their contemporaries without losing their "I" is considered the highest level of development of a nation. This is where the Japanese people excel. Reverence for elders, the duty of a son to his father, to pass on the best to his generation - his uniqueness before the world, that is what characterizes this nation. It is necessary to pay tribute to the fact that today the country remains devoted to its history, and also reverently treating it, tries to preserve and pass on to its children and grandchildren. This attitude to everything that surrounds the Japanese depends on their mentality, worldview, worldview, absorbed into their consciousness over the years and centuries of existence. With the penetration of the West into the land of the Japanese people - the everyday life of the people changed. The clothes changed: kimonos were replaced by European jackets; the army changed weapons: samurai swords were replaced by guns and cannons; railroads appeared, people began to live in a new way. But whatever changed around the Japanese - his consciousness and spirit will remain the same. And today it is the ideology of Tennoism that helps to keep the Japanese people together, not to forget about their roots, traditions and customs.

1.1 The influence of religion on the formation of Japanese ideology

For thousands of years of mankind's existence, religion has been the organizing principle of society. It is a complex social institution, which has absorbed all the richness of folk life, including beliefs, morality, law, aesthetics. Religion largely determines the vectors of people's social behavior. To this day, in almost all societies it continues to be an essential component of their life activity, quite independent of the economy and politics. But it happens that religion becomes an obedient tool in the hands of the ruling elites, who do not stop using it to create an atmosphere of intolerance within the country and to provoke interstate conflicts. In today's world, which is shaken by serious conflicts, many inter-ethnic disputes are rooted in the confrontation of religions.

The surprisingly broad panorama of religious life in modern Japan, where all faiths operate in full harmony, is perhaps one of the few examples worthy of familiarization and study. According to official statistics, the country has 118 million followers of the national religion Shinto, 96 million of Buddhism and 1.5 million Christians (the number of adherents of the so-called new religions cannot be precisely determined), while its population is less than 130 million people. This seemingly paradoxical phenomenon is explained by the fact that the Japanese mostly consider themselves both Shintoists and Buddhists. Both religions have coexisted peacefully in the country for centuries, having divided the human life cycle between them: birth and life are according to the Shinto canons, and funerals - to Buddhism.

This situation is connected with the peculiarities of the historical formation of Japanese religious consciousness. In a broad sense, it is immanent to both the individual and the nation as a whole. Religion as a dogma may disappear, but religious feeling is unusually stable, rising above forms and currents and, at the same time, only fed by the richness of society's intellectual existence. The attitude of the Japanese to religion as a moral value is ambiguous. In the late 1980s, according to public opinion polls, the proportion of believers of different denominations reached 35% of the population. The large number of non-believers, however, cannot be perceived as a lack of religiosity. Such an impression is created if we approach it with Eurocentric norms of belief in one God and eternity of the soul. Recognition of the equality of the two religions - Shinto and Buddhism, as well as the moral and ethical teachings of Confucianism and Taoism, in the opinion of Europeans, indicates the indifference of the Japanese to religion, moreover, their disbelief in general.

In Japan, however, there has never been a single, religious organization subordinating and controlling the whole of human life. And the religious life of the Japanese has never been centered on just one thing. Each family was connected to a Shinto shrine at its place of residence and was assigned to one or another Buddhist temple, according to family tradition. Therefore, one can perhaps define Shinto as a communal religion and Buddhism as a family religion. Many religious rites were performed at home, in the family, without the participation of clerics. The family and the home were the center of religious life. Hence, the Japanese have a tradition of installing altars in the house - Buddhist (butsudan), symbolizing the memory of the deceased and Shinto (kamidana), representing gratitude to the deities. Since antiquity, the Japanese have participated in religious life not as individuals, but as a united family, in other words, the group acted first, and then the individual. The head of a clan or community was both a political leader and a clergyman, directing all the actions of the believers.

The coexistence of religions was postulated as early as the 6th century by Prince Setoku: "there is no contradiction in the three religions. Shinto ... is concerned with the past, not the present or the future. The present is taken care of by the teachings of Confucius, which has, however, the disadvantage of not looking further ahead. Only Buddhism reveals to us the future of man. And since the future is occupied by man, it could not in our country pass Buddhism by." This formula provides a key to understanding how the religious consciousness of the Japanese was shaped and their national character was formed.

The Japanese religious consciousness is based on Shinto, although originally it was not a religion in the strict sense of the word, but a mosaic of various beliefs, cults, rituals and ethical norms. But at the same time, Shinto had a strong irrational but socially powerful side - the cult of ancestors, which reflected the hierarchical structure of real society. This cult formed the basis of the concept of succession, going from demiurgic gods to earthly gods, and from them to legendary emperors and further to the ancestors of the present-day monarch. This idea permeates the historical and literary monument "Records of Ancient Acts" ("Kojiki"), which is, as it is called, the Holy Scripture of Shinto. By endowing monarchs with divine descent from Amaterasu herself, the Kojiki make it possible to establish a strong state cult as a means of the same centralization, general "statehood" of Japan. Kojiki strengthen the position of the central authority historically, politically and religiously. [3, c.535]

Thus, since ancient times, Shinto has had the idea of statehood. The Japanese had come to terms with the legend of the divine origin of their islands and the continuity of the imperial dynasty, which formed one aspect of their religious consciousness.

In ancient Japan there was almost syncretism of Shintoism and Buddhism.[4,p.128] As a result of such coexistence many gods of Shinto began to be endowed with features of Buddhist Bodhisattvas. And the pantheon of Buddhism was replenished with deities of Shintoism. However, despite the consistency of the dogmas of

Buddhism and samurai ethics, there were contradictions between them: Buddhism categorically forbids all murder (the five "great" sins of Buddhism: murder, theft, adultery, lying, and drunkenness). Feudal life in real life demanded just the opposite. Therefore, various kinds of "atonements" (generous donations to temples, tonsure as monks) became popular. At the same time with Buddhism, Confucianism, revised by Zhu Xi, began to spread in Japan. The history of Confucianism in Japan (as well as Taoism) dates back to the early stage of Japanese civilization and statehood. Migrants from the mainland, Chinese and Koreans, brought with them not only Confucian texts, but also the norms of Confucian morality and way of life corresponding to them, as well as many elements of Taoism, which influenced the formation of Shintoism. It is true that Taoism did not strengthen in Japan, although it had a certain influence on some aspects of the way of life and religious practice of the Japanese. In particular, the principles of Taoist protective magic with its spells, amulets, talismans, etc. became widespread in Japan. (Jap. konju), the practice of divination and fortune-telling (bokuso-kikke), and various techniques and principles of Chinese medicine. But Buddhism, which dominated Japan, was quite wary of Taoism, as well as Confucianism (elements of Taoism were more favorably received by Shintoism, which was structurally related to it). Confucianism in Japan, however, unlike Taoism, waited for better times.

From the seventeenth century, when the Tokugawa clan shoguns (1603-1867) succeeded in suppressing the decentralizing tendencies of the Japanese feudal lords and united the country under their rule with an iron hand, when the Buddhist Church led by them became a grass-roots administrative base for keeping the population in obedience, a favorable environment was created for the intensive penetration of Confucianism into Japan.[5, 127c].

The shoguns were counting on Zhu Xi's reformed Neo-Confucianism to give them an additional opportunity to consolidate their power. Confucian ideals of loyalty to those in power, honoring elders, and maintaining the status quo seemed appropriate.

Through the efforts of a number of preachers, Zhushian Neo-Confucianism began to spread rapidly in Japan. The methods of some of the preachers are noteworthy. Yamazaki Ansai (1618-1682), for example, is interesting in this regard. Having been brought up in a monastery, he faced the prospect of expulsion when he became stroppy. Threatening to set fire to the monastery, he frightened the abbot and was abandoned. When Yamazaki grew up, settled down, and, having successfully mastered the basics of Buddhism, became a monk, he became familiar with Confucian texts. The teachings of Confucius in Zhushian interpretation seemed to him the truth, and Yamazaki began to actively preach the ideas of Confucianism, trying to combine the precepts of Confucius and Meng-tzu with the spirit of samurai patriotism and the norms of ancient Shintoism. Typically in the style of Zen masters, he set his students a task-koan: a Chinese army led by Confucius and Meng-tzu invaded Japan. What would you do? The astonished students are silent: brought up in the spirit of patriotism, they understand the need to fight back. But to whom? Confucius?! Yamazaki's answer is simple and instructive: you go into battle, defeat the enemy and take Confucius and Meng-tzu prisoner, to whom, after captivity, you give all the honors due to them as great sages. Thus, the norms of patriotism are observed and the deepest respect is given to these sages. According to Confucius, people were divided into four groups:

1 .People who have wisdom from birth;

2 .People who can acquire wisdom;

3 .People who have difficulty comprehending the teachings;

4 .A people who are unable to learn wisdom or acquire knowledge.

That is, "A sovereign must be a sovereign, a dignitary must be a dignitary, a father must be a father, a son must be a son". This doctrine is more ideological than religious. In Confucianism the concept of God as such is absent at all, and, in fact, Confucianism could properly be called a philosophy rather than a religion. In Japan, Confucianism, merging with Buddhism and Shinto, confirmed the Shinto requirements of "loyalty to duty", obedience and obedience of the subject to his master and emperor; strict observance of the laws of the family, society and state; worship of ancestors. This ensured the support of Confucianism by the feudal rulers of Japan and made this doctrine the basis of education among the ruling class, particularly the samurai. At the heart of Confucianism is the principle of patriarchy, which places filial reverence above all else. There is a large world family consisting of Heaven the father, Earth the mother, and man the child. The second great family is the state family. In it, the emperor is both Heaven and Earth (father and mother), the ministers are his elder sons, the people are his younger sons. And, finally, the ordinary family (clan). The head of each family must command his household and be responsible for them to the state, which recognizes only the family and ignores the individual person. Hence the dogma of loyalty and unquestioning obedience to the father, feudal prince, shogun. Confucianism taught that man becomes a man by virtue of the five virtues (constancy) that distinguish him from the animal:

5 .humanity (the essence of which is love and the manifestation of which is goodness)

2 .justice

3 .good manners (respect for elders, modesty)

4 . wisdom

5 .truthfulness.

If a person, follows the nature of the five permanent virtues, rather than being under the pernicious burden of his natural beginning, the five human relationships arise in his life:

1 . between parents and children;

2 .master and servant;

3 .husband and wife;

4 .older and younger brothers;

5 .between friends.

These five basic relationships were called gorin. For the samurai, the relationship between master and servant was the basic one. The idea of loyalty to the master and the inextricably linked notion of duty were brought to the fore in bushido. Loyalty ("service to the master as the source of all goods") and duty ("realization of this loyalty"). Loyalty to the lord could be expressed not only in constant service to him, readiness at any moment to fall for him. A vassal also showed his loyalty by following his lord on the path of death, which was expressed in "suicide by following", which became by the XIV century a common form of duty fulfillment.

Confucianism in social life has also left many sets of norms of ethical and moral behavior: respect most of all filial respect and brotherly obedience in order to properly raise social relations; treat all relatives generously in order to maintain the spirit of harmony and humility; maintain peace and harmony with neighbors in order to prevent quarrels and litigation; recognize the importance of farming and silk cultivation in order to provide sufficient food and clothing; value moderation and economy in order to prevent wastefulness, r Such dogmas, intensively inculcated for centuries in the consciousness of people, have been deposited in the psychology of the nation in the form of quite definite behavioral stereotypes. It can hardly be said that these dogmas have remained unshakable norms of social regulation in modern Japan, but their importance is indisputable.

Buddhism and especially Zen had a great influence on the development of various aspects of Japanese national culture, and above all on the cultivation of the sense of beauty. Specialists have repeatedly noted that Japanese Buddhism and Buddhists are inclined to hedonism, to enjoyment, to tasting the joys of life to a much greater extent than is generally characteristic of this doctrine and its followers. Apparently, the other-worldly orientation of Japanese culture, noticeable since antiquity and sanctioned by the norms of Shintoism, has influenced Buddhism in this sense. Of course, this influence should not be exaggerated.

Tendencies to hedonism were severely suppressed by education, first of all in Zen schools. However, a peculiar synthesis of the inner - centuries of cultivated ability to admire and enjoy the joys of life and the beauty of existence and the external, stimulated by the official norms of Buddhism striving for austerity and self-restraint created an extremely peculiar aesthetics. Severe austerity and ceremoniousness gave rise to the ability to find hidden beauty in everything, everywhere and always. The art of*interior decoration, the ability to emphasize a line in clothing, and finally, the exquisite ability to arrange a single flower in such a way that the whole room is decorated and illuminated (ikebana), all this is the result of centuries of development of Buddhist aesthetics, mainly Zen aesthetics.

The aesthetics of Zen in Japan are evident in everything. It is in the principles of samurai swordsmanship, in judo techniques, and in the exquisite tea ceremony (shanoyu). This ceremony represents, as it were, the ultimate symbol of aesthetic education, especially for girls from wealthy homes. The ability in a secluded garden, in a specially constructed miniature gazebo, to receive guests, comfortably seat them (in Japanese - on a mat with tucked under himself undressed legs), according to all the rules of art to prepare fragrant green or flower tea, to whisk it with a special whisk, to pour it into tiny cups, to serve it with a graceful bow - all this is the result of a course of Japanese Zen politeness, almost university-like in its capacity and duration (from early childhood).

In general, politeness is one of the characteristic features of the Japanese. It can hardly be attributed only to Zen self-cultivation, although the restraint and dignity, the elegance of Japanese politeness suggest that Zen aesthetics had its influence here as well. Surprisingly, even within bushido, the ruthless sword has always coexisted alongside beauty, refinement, and love. Love - although not chivalrous like medieval European love, but in some ways close to it - played a significant role in the life of the Japanese people. It is not the Confucian-Chinese love for an elder, for a sage, for parents. It is a love sublime, ready for self-sacrifice, sometimes reducing to itself almost the whole meaning of life.[6, p. 213].

But not only Eastern religions were spreading on the territory of Japan. Christianity, a Western religion, also had the opportunity to spread just with the arrival of colonizers. For the first time Japanese people got acquainted with Christianity in the XVI century, when in 1548 together with Spanish merchants three Catholic priests arrived in Japan. They were allowed to worship, which they promptly took advantage of. The missionaries (both the first and subsequent ones) were pleasantly surprised by the attention shown by the Japanese. The visitors thought that the new religion would easily find its way into the hearts of the Japanese. However, it soon became clear that this attention was the result of the fact that tempting goods were arriving along with the missionaries. Local feudal lords encouraged their subjects' contact with the missionaries in every way possible, while receiving overseas offerings. According to some sources, by 1582, 80 Christian missionaries were in Japan and had converted up to fifteen hundred thousand people. It seemed that the ideas of Christ were growing in popularity, but soon the authorities waged a determined struggle against Christianity, even to the point of repressing the missionaries, as well as local converts. In 1614, an edict was issued. By the middle of the 17th century, Christianity in Japan was virtually eliminated.

The second period of its spread did not begin until two hundred years later. In 1859, the first Protestant mission was established in Nagasaki. In Yokohama, Catholic churches were built in 1862 and Protestant churches in 1872. The activities of the missionaries became more and more lively. Toward the end of the nineteenth century, however, they were again persecuted by the authorities and forced to hol up in their missions. After more ups and downs, Christianity retained only a tertiary importance in the country.

It must be said that the Japanese, for the most part, have little knowledge of the intricacies of Christianity. Their pragmatic minds are not inclined toward abstract mystical Christian teaching, but rather they regard it with a kind of distrust and fear. The view gradually developed among the missionaries that Japanese reality was not a good breeding ground for Christianity. Many even tried to explain the stubborn reluctance of the Japanese to accept Christian ideas by the alleged lack of disposition of the Japanese mind to a more complex worldview system than Shintoism, Buddhism, or Confucianism.

Although Christianity has no direct impact on the national psychology of the Japanese, it influences their behavior in an indirect way.

Having analyzed the main religions of the Japanese people, from their spread on the territory of the state to their transformed forms, one cannot help but conclude that Zen Buddhism, Confucianism and Shintoism are the foundations that have formed the worldview, the essence of the Japanese people and the state system of the country. Shinto, with its pantheism and lack of militancy, has shaped the adaptive, religious consciousness of the Japanese. It can provide "information for reflection" on how to influence the formation of religious consciousness in the direction of religious tolerance and non-conflict, which serves as a guarantee of peaceful resolution of inter-confessional conflicts.

The idea of statehood in the Japanese version of Buddhism was combined with the sacredness of imperial power postulated by Shinto, which could not but leave an imprint on the character of Japanese religious consciousness. A great connoisseur of Japan, Lavkadio Hearn, who lived there for many years and adopted not only Buddhism, but also the Japanese name, saw the coexistence of the two major religions as the basis of moral firmness of its population. He wrote: "Japan owes the greatest gratitude to both its religions, the creators and guardians of its moral strength - Shintoism, which teaches that man should think more about the emperor and the state than about himself and his loved ones, and Buddhism, which has cultivated in him the capacity for self-denial, for self-forgetfulness, for patient endurance of suffering and for reconciliation as an immutable law with the loss of everything beloved and dependence on everything hated."[3,p.535].

Confucianism, which brought with it more complex patterns of behavior, norms and rituals, also had a noticeable influence on the religious consciousness of the Japanese. First of all, of course, we are talking about the management of the state, the relationship between the sovereign and his subjects. The assimilation and peaceful coexistence of Shinto, Buddhism and Confucianism were the result of the inherent adaptability of the Japanese worldview.

In the figurative words of historian T. Fujisawa, "Shinto is the roots and trunk, Confucianism is the leaves and branches, and Buddhism is the flowers and fruits". Shintoism and Buddhism exist as organized religions. The former has delivered and preserved the mythologized origins of the country and its people, the canons of shrine construction and the conduct of various kinds of religious and festive activities. The second brought with it the tradition of building lavish temples filled with works of art, as well as memorial services for the departed. With Confucianism came moral and ethical teachings that have had a profound influence on the Japanese cultural tradition.

Over time, the elements of these three religions intertwined and formed a kind of unified whole. The other major religions and religious movements had less significant influence on the warrior class. But soon by the coincidence of the country's history, the time of the shoguns and samurai are again replaced by imperial power. But the ideology of the country, the spirit of the people do not change themselves.... Religious life of modern Japan demonstrates an example of religious tolerance, which is catastrophically lacking in the majority of mankind and which, if widespread enough, could make our planet a much more attractive place to live. The peaceful coexistence of various confessions in the country for centuries already speaks of the influence of religion on the mentality, on the worldview, and the atmosphere of the internal political state in relation to various confessions is stable.

1.2 The cult of the emperor - the ideology of Tennoism

While the term "Tennoism" could formally be translated as "Japanese monarchism," such a translation does not fully reflect the broad and interconnected range of issues associated with the concept of "Tennoism" in Japanese history and modernity. The ideology of tennoism, central to understanding the content of prewar state nationalism (1868-1945), remains viable today in a transformed form. Moreover, the values of this ideological system, which is based on an official reinterpretation of archaic myths, serve as a key to understanding many features of the Japanese national character, their worldview, socio-political perceptions, and socio-cultural orientations. In short, "tennoism" is a complex multidimensional phenomenon of life in Japanese society, which has its own internal laws of development, which are not at all easy to understand. [7, c.7]

Mass veneration of the emperor was consciously cultivated (through the state Shintoism) by the rulers of the Meiji era (1868-1912), who saw in the imperial throne the only reliable support in the consolidation of the nation in the conditions of backwardness and weakness of Japan, which was threatened by the loss of national independence. But while forming the system of Tennoist views, the official ideologists skillfully wove into it deeply rooted in the national ethical and political thought, the dogmas of Shintoism, the principles of Confucianism, Taoism, Buddhist philosophy, and ancient folk ideas and beliefs. The ideological justification of royal power in ancient Japan was based primarily on the traditions of the local religion - Shintoism. The royal family was considered to have a special magical power that ensured effective communication with the deities, without which the prosperous functioning of the entire social organism was unthinkable. "Three divine regalia" as embodying the virtues of the emperor and members of his family: mirror - honesty, sword - wisdom, jasper pendants - mercy. Only the emperor could rule the country, making these virtues the main principles of policy. Hence the basis of the morality of the people in "keeping loyalty to the supreme ruler, even if one has to sacrifice one's life for it." This sacral significance of royal power caused the royal family to retain its supreme position in the hierarchical structure of society, despite the fact that it was excluded by other noble families from the real business of governing the social units consolidated into the state organism.

After the struggle between the supporters of the shogunate and the advocates of the restoration of imperial power in favor of the latter, the new government faced the task of accelerated economic and military strengthening of the country, formulated by Meiji leaders in the form of the slogan of creating a "rich country and strong army" (fu-koku kyohei). The need to accomplish this task in the shortest possible time was necessitated by the pressure of Western powers and the threat of losing the country's national independence.

The new rulers of Japan found themselves in a difficult situation. On the one hand, it was clear that without modernizing all aspects of society according to the Western model, without reorganizing it on a new basis, it would be extremely difficult to solve the task at hand. On the other hand, excessive enthusiasm for Western sciences and ideas was fraught with the loss of the identity of Japanese culture, the disintegration of the integrity of the emerging national organism. Moreover, only the most educated strata of Japanese society were ready for a deep, essential perception of the new in Western forms, and at the mass level, the desire to learn from the West often led to an ugly adoration of the achievements of a higher civilization, to superficial copying of purely external manifestations of an unfamiliar culture, which were striking in their novelty. Under such conditions, Meiji political leaders, after twenty years of cautious search for a balanced approach to the development of concrete ways of restructuring, refused to radically break the traditional moral foundations of society, and took a course to transform the use of traditional stereotypes of religious consciousness, which were rooted and accessible to the perception of the masses.

Measures were taken to ensure that borrowings from foreign cultures were of a purely utilitarian and applied nature and did not affect the spiritual foundations of the Japanese nation. As they said in Japan at that time, the development of the country was to combine "Japanese spirit and European knowledge" (wakon yosai). Of course, such a compromise solution carried the danger of many contradictory clashes, and yet, paradoxically, it seems that this was the path that ensured Japan's survival and rapid modernization. To achieve the unity of the nation, to win the masses ideologically, to solve the problem of their political activation under the control of the government, taking into account the socio-political and cultural-psychological peculiarities of the mass consciousness of that time, it was possible only by creating a cementing ideology that combined both religious and nationalistic principles. The ideology of Tennoism, which retained many elements rooted in religious traditions, corresponded to these conditions.

Another characteristic feature of Shinto was its blatant nationalistic orientation. At the same time, in violation of the religious tradition of religious tolerance (the Japanese had long worshipped numerous deities of different religions simultaneously, often separating them only functionally), the rise of Shinto in its state form was accompanied by oppression of other religious movements. Only one of the gods was now required to be favored, namely the "living god," the emperor. Over the next eight decades, until 1945, the ideology of Tennoism underwent certain changes and became more complex, but it can be characterized by a number of nodal points that are fundamental for the entire period.

The main points of the ideology of Tennoism

The core of the ideology of Tennoism is a set of concepts, usually denoted in Japanese literature by the difficult-to-translate word "kokutai"'. Orientalist T.P. Grigorieva defines this notion as "the moral basis of a social organism" and explains: "In Japan, for centuries, the idea of the state as a complex organism, a continuum, whose life is conditioned by a certain type of connection of everything with everything, was formed. Everything was bound together not by law and not by the constitution, but by Heaven, i.e. by the laws of nature itself, realized in specific ethical principles. So, traditional morality, from the point of view of the Japanese, is that which directly links the individual parts among themselves, that to which the nation owes its integrity" [3, pp. 4-5] [3, c. 4-5]. G.E. Svetlov, believing that the translation of the word "kokutai" as "national state system" does not sufficiently convey the extremely capacious content of this term, suggests using the successfully found descriptive translation of "kokutai" proposed by J. Spa: "unique (Japanese) national essence" [7, p. 140]. [7, c. 140]. This translation most fully reveals the peculiarity of the interpretation of "kokutai" by official nationalist ideologists as a concept encompassing political, moral, religious, historical and geographical features of Japan - the "divine country". The central element of "kokutai" was considered to be the idea of a mystical bond between the emperor and the Japanese people. It was this bond that was recognized as the foundation of the Japanese state and nation in official nationalist literature throughout the period from the Meiji Revolution to the end of World War II.

The main components of the "kokutai" structure are the myth of the "divine" origin of the Japanese state (or the concept of the "spirit of the foundation of the state"), the myth of the "divine" virtues of the emperor and the "unique" moral qualities of Japanese subjects ("Japanese spirit"), and, finally, the myth of the "great mission of the nation". In Tennoist ideology, references to forces beyond human comprehension - to divine providence - constantly appeared. The Japanese state, according to the official version, arose by the will of the main goddess of the Shinto pantheon - the sun goddess Amaterasu, she laid the foundations of the throne, which was therefore declared as "eternal and indestructible as Heaven and Earth". Here is one of the typical statements of the official propaganda: "In the great sacred will and great sacred acts of the emperor - an incarnate deity, the great divine will of the imperial ancestors is manifested (meaning the ancestress of the imperial dynasty - the goddess Amaterasu and the imperial ancestors. - T.S.-N.), and their will determines the infinite future of our nation" [27, c. 183].

Thus, the myth of the emperor's "divine" origin is based on the Shinto postulate that the imperial dynasty is related by blood to the sun goddess Amaterasu. This myth was legitimized in the Imperial Constitution of 1889, Article 1 of which reads: "The Japanese Empire shall be ruled forever and ever by an imperial dynasty." And Art. 3 adds: "The Imperial person is sacred and inviolable." "Sacred" imperial dynasty forms the basis of "kokutai" in the Tennoist system. The dogma of the "divinity and continuity of the imperial dynasty" (banshei ikkei) is joined by the myth of the virtues of the emperor, who realizes the great ideal of the goddess Amaterasu, embodied in the "three divine regalia" of the Japanese dynasty - jasper pendants, mirror and sword. Tennoist ideologists usually refer to the chronicle and mythological codex "Nihon seki", which records the presentation of these regalia to the first ruler of Japan by the goddess Amaterasu. The emperor has the virtues of the goddess Amaterasu herself, so imperial rule cannot be inherently unrighteous. The Japanese subjects were thus led to believe that the emperor was infallible in all matters of religion, politics, and morality because he possessed an inscrutable, mystical divinity that allowed him to see the true path of his country and subjects without error. This path, called the "kodo" ("imperial path"), was interpreted by the Japanese preachers of Tennoism as the ideal of the Japanese state.

Shintoist ideas of the emperor's "divinity" were used by official propaganda as a spiritual basis for the formation of a clear sense of national identity centered in veneration of the emperor. Here is an excerpt from an article by General S. Araki (1877-1966), one of the militaristic ideologues of Tennoism, answering the question he posed himself, with what the Japanese identity is associated: "It is nothing else but the great ideal represented by the three regalia of the Japanese dynasty (jasper pendants, mirror and sword), which Amaterasu handed over at the founding of the Japanese state.... Mercy, justice and courage, represented by the three regalia of the Japanese dynasty, are the ideal of the Japanese state, the path of which was pointed out by the emperors.... The history of Japan represents precisely the movement along this path. It is the duty of the Japanese nation - a nation of loyal subjects of His Majesty - to preserve it, to glorify it." One of the main principles of Tennoism throughout its existence was the principle of "saisei itchi" ("unity of ritual and state administration"). It was adopted immediately after the Meiji Revolution and repeatedly emphasized in the imperial edicts as "the fundamental principle of "kokutai" and national community since the establishment of the Japanese state" [26, p. 143] [26, c. 143]. It was thanks to the principle of "saisei itti" that the subjects of the Japanese Empire could realize "kokutai" and "the great way of honoring the gods" [26, p. 144] [26, c. 144]. The content of the principle of "saisei itti" is revealed most fully from known sources in the official pamphlet published in 1937 and called "Basic Principles of Kokutai" ("Kokutai no hongi"): "The emperor, through the practice of religious rituals, becomes one with his divine ancestors and, merging with their spirit, can lead his subjects and multiply their prosperity.

Thus, the divinity of the emperors who rule the country is manifested. Therefore, the emperor's veneration of the gods and his ruling of the state are essentially one. The emperor transmits the divine precepts of his ancestors and thus clarifies the great principle of the founding of the nation and the great path that the subjects should follow. ...In other words, the education of subjects is inseparable from religious rituals and the administration of the state" [27, p. 187]. [27, c. 187]. The ideology of Tennoism also used the traditional Japanese concept of "harmonious state", adopting native Japanese worldview attitudes. Of the "five great ethical attitudes", the observance of which, according to Confucianism, guaranteed the harmonious development of society, Tennoism exalted above all the special, peculiar only to "divine" Japan, relations between the emperor and his subjects, which consisted in the unity of the highest with the lowest - the monarch with his people. In the Shinto ideas about the "divine", bearing visible traces of the cult of ancestors, there is no clear distinction between "kami" (deities) and man, they are in a certain sense united, as a parent and a child are united. This put a serious imprint on the Confucian ethical and political principles of the absolute power of the emperor - it was the relationship between parents and children that was considered in Japan as the prototype of social organization, as a model for all other social relations, and loyalty to the emperor was placed above filial reverence. The Tennoist ideologists never tired of repeating that the genealogy of the Japanese goes back to a single root.

The Japanese nation was thus viewed as one big family, and the emperor did not act as a militant theocratic ruler imposing norms of behavior on his subjects in all areas of life by force, but as the spiritual head of the nation who protected all Japanese without distinction. The emperor, fatherly loving and protective, led his subjects, whom he treated as "omitakara" (lit. "great treasure," but meaning rather "beloved subjects"), along the true path pointed out by the goddess Amaterasu. The subjects were taught that the fatherly feeling of the emperor surpasses the love of parents for their children: the emperor with "great divine mercy forgives the misdeeds of his subjects" [27, p. 185-189]. In return for such patronage, the emperor had to arouse in his subjects feelings of loyalty and gratitude for favors, like other Shinto "kami". As a result, the moral and political duty of the Japanese acquired the force of an inner unconscious impulse toward grateful obedience, the realization of which generated a sense of inner satisfaction. In other words, loyalty to the emperor, equated with patriotism, was inculcated by the Shinto faith and became a kind of inner need of every Japanese, especially as Tennoist propaganda became truly national in scope. This special Japanese attitude toward duty has been noted by many Japanese scholars. For example, Professor K. Mizushima of Rissho University believes that the Japanese concept of debt to society is fundamentally different from the European one, because it (debt) is caused not by a socially conditioned obligation, but by the feeling of appreciation, gratitude as a purely subjective motivation of the soul [28, p. 196-197].

The Tennoist doctrine of the "harmonious state" was thus based on the nationalist interpretation of the Shinto view of the harmonious relationship between the divine and the human. This justified the endowment of the Japanese with unique innate virtues, manifesting themselves on the sole condition that the subjects serve the emperor's cause in a united impulse, selflessly, i.e., in Japanese terminology, achieve "tukun" ("sincerity of heart in honoring the emperor"). This is what the mentioned pamphlet "Kokutai no hongi" says: "Wherever the virtue of the emperor's mercy is extended, the path of the subjects becomes clear by itself. This way of subjects is realized when the whole nation, united in heartfelt impulse, serves the emperor..... This means that from birth we serve the emperor and follow the way of the Empire, and it is quite natural that we, the subjects, possess such an important quality " [27, c. 189]. "Loyalty means honoring the emperor as the source of everything and obeying him completely. To follow the path of loyalty is the only way of life possible for us subjects; this path is the source of all energy. Consequently, to give our lives in the name of the emperor means not so-called self-sacrifice, but overcoming our small selves in the name of life under the divine imperial protection" [27, p. 190] [27, c. 190].

The nationalists considered "Western individualism and rationalism" to be the most significant obstacle to the "path of loyalty," and under this category fell a very wide range of Western ideology, from the ideas of bourgeois enlightenment to Marxist doctrine. Only by honoring the Shinto gods and, above all, the "living god" (arahito gami) - the emperor - could a Japanese, according to official propaganda, follow the "path of loyalty" identified with patriotism. In other words, Tennoism reinforced loyalty with Shinto faith modified in the interests of the state, the original traditional moral values, and equated such "sacred" loyalty with patriotism. Loyalty, understood in unity with the veneration of Shinto gods and the fulfillment of patriotic duty, became one of the cornerstones of state Shintoism. It is loyalty in the above sense, according to the tennoism's tenets, that forms the basis of Japan's harmonious development, unparalleled in world history. "The hearts of the subjects, following the united path of loyalty and filial reverence, merging with the great august merciful heart of the emperor, grow the fruits of harmony between the monarch and his subjects, which predetermines the endless future of our nation" [27, p. 196]. [27, c. 196].

According to Tennoism, these special, harmonious, conflict-free relations between kami and people, between nature and man, between family members, between superiors and inferiors, and between emperor and subjects had musubi as their source. This Shinto term denotes the mystical creative energy that was most fully manifested during the creation of the Japanese islands by the divine couple Izanagi and Izanami, underlying the development of all things, phenomena, beings, including the Japanese nation. This is where Tennoism comes close to formulating the "Japanese spirit": "In our country, differences of opinion or interests stemming from differences of status are easily overcome through a unique harmony that draws from a single source. In everything, it is not struggle that is the ultimate goal, but harmony; everything bears fruit rather than dying by being destroyed. This is the great spirit of our nation" [27, c. 199]. Only selfless service to the emperor enabled the Japanese to realize fully their potential virtues. The culmination of harmony was proclaimed to be the sacrifice of the subjects' lives to the emperor. In doing so, he acquired "kiyoki kokoro" ("purity of heart"), or "magokoro" ("truthfulness of heart"), which equaled purification, the main and most ancient Shinto rite.

Another myth on which the "unique national essence" in the interpretation of Tennoist ideology rested was the myth of the "heavenly destiny" (temmei) of the Japanese nation, called by the gods themselves, primarily by the goddess Amaterasu, to "save mankind" and "establish harmony" throughout the world by extending the power of the "godly Tenno" to it. The ideologists of Tennoism operated with references to classical Shinto literature, and above all to the myths of the Nihon Seki, which they interpreted on the basis of quite earthly objectives of the wars of conquest of imperialist Japan. The Japanese were brought up to believe that from the time immemorial when the Japanese state was founded by the goddess

Amaterasu, when the first emperor, Jimmu, came to the throne, and throughout Japanese history, the social activities of the tenno subjects were subordinated to the fulfillment of Amaterasu's sacred mission to extend the "divine" rule over ever-widening territories. To support this claim, official propaganda usually quoted (from the Nihon Seki) a statement of the mythical Emperor Jimmu before the so-called eastern campaign, as well as Emperor Jimmu's edict on his accession to the throne after six years of wars to pacify unruly tribes in the east of the Japanese Islands. In the edict, Emperor Jimmu vowed to the goddess Amaterasu to "extend imperial power to the whole world so as to gather the eight corners under one roof (hakko iti u)." This slogan, often also translated as "the whole world is one family" or "the whole world under one roof," was regarded by official Tennoism as a divine imperative.

The preachers of militant "Japanism" argued that only the Japanese, endowed with the virtues of the "Japanese spirit" through "racial purity and unity," were capable of "spreading the light of their culture to all mankind," for "the heavenly purpose of the Japanese state" (nihonkoku no tammei) was to create a single new culture for all mankind. It was the propaganda of the "divine" mission of "hakko itti u" that gave the expansionist actions of Japanese imperialism on the A'iat continent (beginning with the Japanese-Chinese war of 1894-1895 and ending with aggressive actions in 1931-1945) the character of a "holy war" in the eyes of ordinary Japanese. The slogan "hakko itti u" was also used to justify Japan's special rights to lead the peoples of the "yellow race" in liberating them from the yoke of the Western powers. The ethnocentrism inherent in Shinto mythology was developed by the ideologists of Tennoism into a theory of racial superiority, which justified the rights of the Japanese to dominate all other races and peoples who were not protected by the Shinto gods.

Tennoist ideas formed the basis of the Japanese version of pan-Asianism, which became more and more sophisticated as Japan's military expansion in Asia expanded. Japanese pan-Asianists created a peculiar hierarchical system of ethnic values based on the quasi-family principle, according to which the Japanese nation, armed with the ideals of the "Yamato race" or the "high principles" of the "eight corners under one roof," stood at the head of the family of Asian peoples and was called upon to rule over the backward, amorphous peoples of other Asian countries. The peoples of Western and Soviet states were declared "barbarians" and cultural antipodes, alien to the Asian community of peoples. The dominant position of the "white race" in Asia was to be rightfully ceded to the Japanese - the "Yamato race", which surpassed all others in its biological and ethno-psychological merits. One of the ideologists of the "kokutai", S. Uesugi, who as early as 1919 claimed that "the salvation of all human civilization is the mission of the Japanese Empire", wrote: "At present the nations of the world know no order. They are divided into classes, each of which fights only for its own interests and regards the other class as an irreconcilable enemy. Radicalism is spreading abroad. The poison of this disease is penetrating flesh and blood and threatens to topple nations.... The heart of man has lost the capacity for cooperation. Individuals do as they please, acting without restraint ... The whole world is torn by the struggle between capital and labor.... There is an inferno of struggle and bloodshed on earth.... There is not a single person among the Japanese people who does not believe that, if only they had our emperors, they would not have reached such an extreme situation.... Our people, thanks to the divine virtues of the emperors, have been endowed with such national foundations of statehood as have no analogy in the whole world.... And if the whole world could now live under the auspices of our emperor's virtues, the light of hope for a humanistic future could be kindled. Only in this way can the world be saved from destruction. Only in this way is life in a world of goodness and beauty possible. Truly great is the mission of our nation" [6, c. 82].

As if to continue Uesugi's reasoning, the Taisho nichi nichi shimbun newspaper wrote: "Our people and the gods ... seek only to fulfill this greatest and noblest task of uniting the world under the Emperor of Japan. Our main goal is to extend the rule of the Emperor of Japan to the whole world, as he is the only ruler in the world who fulfills the spiritual mission inherited from his divine ancestors." According to the tenets of the monarchical cult of Tennoism, the main force called upon to fulfill "hakko itti u" was the Japanese imperial army, or, in Tennoist terminology, "the sacred host sent by Heaven to bring life to all things." Japanese warriors, from the highest officers to ordinary soldiers, fulfilling their military duty, became "one in spirit with the divine emperor" and joined the Shinto "kami". Harmony was proclaimed as a property inherent in the "sacred warrior spirit" of the Japanese, supposedly existing not "to kill men, but to give them life." "This warrior spirit seeks to give life to all things, it does not seek destruction.

In other words, it is a struggle based on peace with the promise of new growth and development .... War in this sense is in no way intended for destruction, subjugation and suppression of others, it serves the realization of great harmony, peace, helping to reveal the life-giving power of musubi" [27, p. 197]. A somewhat more modern interpretation of the special mission of the Japanese was contained in the theories of the Kyoto school of philosophy headed by the prominent philosopher K. Nishida. In his work, Nishida put forward a nationalist theory of the state and nation, which was based on the apologetics of a special morality "kokutai", sanctified by the high principles of the "imperial way", praising the Japanese nation as an "energetic, active force" designed to "shape" the Asian nations, which were only passive material in the construction of the "new world order". This theory gave the traditional postulates of Japanese nationalism the appearance of modern science, since it was created on the basis of a combination of the ideological arsenal of the latest idealistic currents of Western countries with traditional Eastern teachings. Openly racist ideas about the chosenness of the "Yamato race" fed the theory of the "sphere of common prosperity in Great East Asia", put forward during the Second World War by representatives of the most reactionary wing of the Kyoto School, M. Kosaka, I. Koyama and others. Japan. According to this theory, Japan was an example of a national community with "harmonious relations", as it was based on the "unique national essence" ("kokutai") with its unity of the emperor and the people.

The idea of such a community was to be carried by Japan to the countries of East Asia and to create with them a single inter-ethnic community based on the "national kinship" of the peoples of these countries. Japanese culture was assigned a leading role in building the culture of the entire region, which would be characterized by an "Oriental humanism" that would make it possible to overcome the crisis of bourgeois society. Japanese culture was attributed to the "special, pure moral energy of the Japanese spirit" and the ideals of "eight corners under one roof".

Tennoism thus addressed the Japanese as the superior human race, developing its concept of a "chosen people." A racial myth was created, coupled with the cult of the emperor, a Shinto ritualistic religious system. The ideologists of Tennoism apparently realized the need to give the official ideology the form of a social myth, since the mass consciousness of the Japanese, especially in the first decades after the Meiji Revolution, was clearly drawn to mythological forms of worldview. Mythmaking in general is characteristic of any person when he or she experiences his or her national belonging as well as belonging to bygone generations.

In Japan, the effectiveness of the impact of the religious mythology of Tennoism was hundredfold increased due to the long cultivation of mythmaking among the Japanese by the Shinto faith. Unlike Western countries in Japan, the process of modernization did not change the ways of moral regulation of social life. In post-Meiji Japan, a layer of pre-bourgeois (traditional) type of social communication was dominant, so the system of religious replenishment of reality could not help but retain its traditional form adapted to new conditions and tasks. "Rational way of thinking was far from penetrating into the life of the majority of the population, its environment was rather dominated by superstition and unscientific way of thinking" [22, c.197].

On the basis of ancient Shinto mythology, a social mythology was created that actively used traditional spiritual values and various symbolism of mythological themes as a means of national integration, stabilization of social relations and mobilization of emotional and moral regulators of human relations in Japanese society. The myths of tennoism were designed to sanctify quite concrete, earthly, not "otherworldly" moments of social life - issues of political power and public duty, military expansion, preservation of national identity and unity, etc. National limitation was not overcome, but cultivated and sanctified along with the sacralization of the existing social orders of the imperial system. In the ideological and image complex of Tennoism there is an intertwining of the mythical and the real, which finds its expression in the moral and political principles of social relations put forward by this ideology. The authors of Tennoist concepts assigned to the ideology protective functions in relation to the state of the imperial system.

The Japanese state was presented as an emanation of higher powers, which provided it with a status of legitimacy in the eyes of the masses. The ruling circles ruled not in their own name, but in the name of the emperor, who personified the state, which was identified with the nation.

Thus, Japanese subjects were not subject to ordinary mortals, but to some mysterious authority surrounded by a mystical halo of sacredness. Tennoist ideology was designed to insinuate that, despite certain differences, the Japanese, as a "divine nation," had formed, since the mythical founding of the state in 660 B.C., a community united by a common destiny ordained by the Shinto gods. This exploited the religious notion that the fate of the community depended on the will of the deities, who blessed the behavior of the entire nation or left its members without their patronage. The condition for following the "path with the gods" (kannagara) was the immutability and Confucian eternity of the emperor's rule, who was like a medium between the divine and the earthly.

The ideologists' interpretation of Japanese history as the result of "divine Providence" sanctified the Confucian ideas of loyalty and obedience and sacralized the object of loyalty, when in the Japanese mind the concepts of "emperor," "state," and "nation" were identified. In other words, Tennoism elevated the doctrine of Japan's unique social order to the degree of Shinto dogma, elevating it to the level of religious faith, which deprived the possibility of a critical attitude to the attitudes of Tennoism and did not allow any changes in the "kokutai". Emphasizing the common interests of all Japanese combined with a nationalistic opposition to all other peoples as inferior, devoid of "divine" blessing, made Tennoism an exceptionally effective ideology in terms of uniting the Japanese nation on the basis of a synthesis of renewed traditional religious ideology and modern bourgeois nationalism.

Thus, having analyzed the factor of religion of the Japanese people in the formation and formation of their national consciousness, ideology, and national spirit, we come to the conclusion that the cementing basis of national ideology is not one religion, as is generally accepted, but three. All three religions - Shinto, Buddhism and Confucianism - have equally laid the foundations of Japanese identity, worldview and national spirit. And the state system is based on the tenets and postulates of the Shinto religion, on which the ideology of Tennoism - the cult of imperial power - was built. The ideology of Tennoism is, up to the present day.

Chapter 2: Shaping the Political Priorities of Postwar Japan

Post-war Japan embarked on the path of building a democratic society. Taking the Western model of development as a basis, while preserving its national identity, the country successfully overcame both economic and political difficulties of the late 40s and early 50s, gradually approaching the classical model of democracy. Emperor Hirohito of Japan, at a press conference held in 1977, trying to explain some of the points of his New Year's address of 1946 (known as the "Declaration of Man"), noted that the adoption of democracy in Japan occurred not so much under American control, but as a result of realizing it as a historical necessity. "We adopted democracy because it was the wish of Emperor Meiji..... The Meiji Constitution is built on that basis, and so I think it was imperative to show that democracy is not something imported" [29,p 252].

However, when speaking about real democracy in Japan, we should not forget that it has never been peculiar to the political culture of this country, which is also characteristic of other states in the area of Confucianism. Despite the attempt to transition to democracy during the Meiji period, serious changes in Japan's political system occurred only after its defeat in World War II. At the same time there was no loss of traditions and national identity, because the political elite showed maximum pragmatism and realistically assessed the situation. [30, c.161]

The uniqueness of the Japanese experience was noted by Samuel Huntington: "Western civilization is both Western and modern. Non-Western civilizations have tried to become modern without becoming Western. So far, only Japan has been completely successful in this" [31, p.51] The state authorities, using Tennoism, are building a new national idea, which will be able to unite the Japanese people for the further development of the country.

2.1 Tennoism - a new national idea. The Imperial House - "yesterday" and "today"

Emperor of Japan

The origin of the Japanese imperial house is shrouded in oddities, legends and prejudices. Here is at least one amazing fact: the ruling dynasty has not been interrupted for at least one and a half thousand years. Another fact: unlike European monarchs, unlike all other Japanese families, houses, clans and clans, the imperial house has no surname - a thing unthinkable for Europe. The position of the ruling house in Japan was so peculiar and strong that it simply did not need any surname.[32, p.25].

The figure of the Japanese "emperor" was sacred. But it was a different kind of sacredness from Europe. It was a kind of inviolability - in the sense that the Japanese emperor did not become the subject of pictorial or verbal representation, or did so to a minimal degree. The Japanese emperor resembles a Shinto deity, who is generally never depicted either. With the exception of ancient mythological and chronicle vaults, we have extremely little "living" evidence to assist us in portraying Japanese rulers.

In ancient times, the ruler of Yamato (Japan) was simply called "great lord" (ookimi). If there were lords (kimi), there was a great lord among them. That is, the ruler was "merely" the first among equals. However, as the territory of the state expanded and the authority of the ruling family increased, a symbolic justification of this position was increasingly required.

The Japanese rulers of ancient times had at least three names: child, adult, and posthumous. From the ideological point of view, the most important was the multicomponent posthumous name, which best reflected what the ruling elite wanted to instill in itself, and at the same time in everyone else. The posthumous name of Emperor Temmu includes the following word combination, which is directly related to Chinese political thought: Heavenly Sage from Oki (Oki no Mahito), - one of the three sacred Taoist mountains, where immortal sages dwelt. The earthly emperor was thus likened to a heavenly divine lord. That is why the imperial edicts so often used the expression "kamunagara" - "Being a deity". The ruler's throne room was called either the "purple palace" (purple being the most sacred color) or the "Hall of the Great Limit". The concept of the Great Limit expressed the idea of the ultimate state of being, from which the feminine and masculine beginnings, and then the whole being, are born by successive doubling.

The attributes of imperial power in Japan are sword, mirror and jasper seal. Iron swords and bronze mirrors are found in abundance during excavations of ancient burial mounds, i.e. they were already believed to have sacred power. The seal throughout the Far East is an attribute of certain powers. Earlier, before the onset of comprehensive Chinese influence, the role of the seal was performed by the magatama - a plate of semi-precious stone, made in the shape of a comma. All three regalia are handed down from generation to generation when a new emperor ascends the throne.

The coat of arms of the Imperial House is a sixteen-petaled chrysanthemum. It is often depicted as a modern state symbol - for example, on foreign passports. In Japanese culture, the chrysanthemum was considered a sign of longevity, due to the chrysanthemum's known resistance to cold weather. Legend reports that, near a river on a rock grew a lot of chrysanthemums. Dew from the flowers rolled into the water, and those people who drank water from the river, were distinguished by excellent health and longevity. Hence the belief that wine infused with chrysanthemum petals extends life up to 8,000 years.

The ruling family of Japan considered itself a descendant of the main deity of the Shinto pantheon, Amaterasu. The dominant position of this family was originally conditioned by kinship with the deity of the sun. It was blood kinship that provided the emperor and his descendants with the throne, all other considerations played no role. None of the possible rivals of the imperial family could claim that, in case of overthrow of the ruling house, someone would recognize him as the legitimate sovereign. Therefore, attempts to overthrow the emperor are also almost non-existent in Japanese history.

Up until the Meiji Renewal, the order of succession in Japan was not defined. At present, the throne is passed only through the direct male line. Until then, any representative of the ruling family could theoretically become emperor or empress. Therefore, the childlessness of the emperor or the absence of sons in his offspring did not lead to the interruption of the dynasty, as it happened in European and Russian history. Nevertheless, it was still considered preferable for direct male heirs of the ruling tenno to take the throne.

With very few exceptions, the Japanese emperor never possessed the full range of commanding powers that his European and Russian monarchical counterparts possessed. Thus, the appearance of the Japanese emperor in the theater of war as supreme commander-in-chief seems quite impossible. The tenno does not leave the confines of the capital, does not travel either within the country or, even more so, abroad, since the main function of the tenno is to stay in the sacral center, i.e. in the palace. The emperor participates in the rituals as the chief priest of Shinto, he is worshipped as a living deity, but he is obliged to maintain ritual purity and therefore does not touch worldly affairs. The very fact that he is on the throne is the surest guarantee that things are going well in the country.

The emperor's other most important function was speech, since it was in his name that decrees were proclaimed. Another function of the emperor was time management, a task that in ancient societies was usually performed by priests. The calendars drawn up at the end of the year were distributed to all institutions and provinces on behalf of the ruler. Thus, it was the emperor who was the "master" of the future time and regulated its course. The emperor also had the right to rename the motto before the expiration of his term of office. No purely ecclesiastical calendars existed in the country. The emperor exercised control over the past time with the help of annals - it was at his command that they were compiled by officials, not by monarchs, as was the custom in Russia.

The structure of Japanese power over the last thousand and fifteen hundred years has been such that the real commanding power has almost always been vested not in the emperor himself, but in another person or institution, making the tenno fundamentally invulnerable to any criticism that might be directed at him. In antiquity it was the head of the family. In medieval times it was the military rulers, the shoguns, who were formally appointed by sovereign decree. In modern times, the function of governing the country was assumed by the parliament and the government.

The current status of the emperor, which the constitution adopted after the end of World War II defines as a symbol of the unity of the nation, fits in well with historical realities. All sociological surveys show that there are extremely few people who would be in favor of abolishing the institution of tenno.[32, p.73].

The defeat of Japanese militarism in 1945 and the democratic transformation of society that followed meant a significant undermining of the official ideology of Tennoism. In the first post-war period, under the influence of the unprecedented rise of the democratic movement under the control of the American occupation authorities, a course was pursued to eradicate the main manifestations of militarism and Tennoism, to debunk the myths about the "divine" origin of the emperor and Japan. These measures were stipulated in the Potsdam Declaration of 1945, as well as in the directive of the occupation authorities, handed to the Japanese government on December 15, 1945, on the separation of the Shinto religion from the state.

Among the steps taken to implement the course of the victorious allies against militarism and Tennoism, first of all, we should name the emperor's renunciation of his "divine" origin in his New Year's address to the people in 1946, the democratic reform of education, which abolished "moral education" in the spirit of Tennoism in schools, and finally, the adoption of a new, democratic constitution in 1947, which transferred sovereignty in the country to the people. The power of the emperor, according to the constitution, was given a nominal character - it was limited to the status of "symbol of the state and unity of the nation". This was the basis for the designation of the postwar state system in Japanese literature as the "Shocho Tennosei" - "symbolic imperial system".

These and other reforms of Japan's social structure, although marking a qualitatively new stage in the country's development, were not entirely consistent in undermining the religious roots of state nationalism. For example, the directive on the separation of Shinto from the state still allowed the emperor to be portrayed as the spiritual head of the country and gave him the right to make pilgrimages to Shinto temples accompanied by state officials, although formally as a private person. The emperor's denial of his "divine" origin began with a long quotation from Emperor Meiji's "Oath" of 1869, which, according to Hirohito, was to serve henceforth as "the basis of national policy" [6, pp. 179-180] [6, c. 179- 180]). The inconsistency and contradiction in the policy of democratization of post-war Japan is also evidenced by the attempt to combine the principles of constitutional monarchy with the principle of popular sovereignty, which is still the reason for discussions among Japanese legal scholars about the nature of the state system of the country. The decisive course to abandon the traditions of nationalist ideology was also hindered by the fact that, as the American journalist M. Gain wrote, "the implementation of democratization was entrusted to a non-democratic government" [6, p. 191]. [6,c. 191]. Moreover, in the policy of the American occupation authorities already by the spring of 1946 there was a turn to curtail many areas of democratic restructuring of Japan. In April 1946, General MacArthur's headquarters received a secret order from the Committee for the Coordination of Foreign, Military, and Naval Affairs in Washington, D.C., which pointed out the danger of strengthening the position of the Communists if a republic was established in Japan and gave instructions on how to preserve the imperial system. MacArthur was ordered to "secretly promote the popularization of the Emperor's personality not as a being of divine origin, but as a human" [6, c. 201-202]. All this contributed to the fact that immediately after the adoption of the 1947 constitution, the ruling circles launched a massive ideological campaign for the preservation of "kokutai". Apparently, considering the democratic reforms only as a temporary concession and intending to immediately begin activities to emasculate the democratic content of the transformations in the system of state power by interpreting them in the spirit of pre-war attitudes. As Prime Minister Shigeru Yoshida stated during the discussion of this issue at the parliamentary session, the new provision on "the emperor as a symbol of the state and the unity of the nation" coincides with the long-established in the minds of the Japanese people the idea that the emperor symbolizes Japanese statehood, and does not contradict the traditional views on the monarchical rule in the country as "the form of the Japanese state that emerged naturally" [32, p. 67]. [32, c. 67].

Thus, immediately after the abolition of the imperial system enshrined in the Meiji Constitution, the search for and development of a new formulation of tennoism in accordance with the changed situation began. The term "kokutai" eventually disappeared from official doctrine, but this did not mean that the nationalist attitudes embodied in the term were completely abandoned.

From the spring of 1946, government-controlled activities began to restore the emperor's prestige and to adapt him to his new role under the new conditions. The process of revitalization of Tennoism after the constitution of 1947 came into force can be divided into three main stages.

The first stage can be conventionally designated by the time frame of the late 40s - the first half of the 60s. This was the period of the lowest fall of the emperor's prestige. In general, from the point of view of the revival of Tennoism, this twenty-year period can be characterized as a time of searching for new means, forms and methods of using the "symbolic imperial system" and testing them in the official policy of ideological and psychological influence on the masses. The ideological formulation of the cult of the emperor did not take the form of a detailed concept, but was limited to the popularization of a "new" image of the emperor, uninvolved in politics, standing above all classes and strata of Japanese society. Ways were sought to establish and strengthen ties between the emperor, who had renounced his "divine" origin, and his former subjects, who had become sovereign citizens, modified from the period of militarism. Conditions were slowly being created in the country for the revival of the cult of the emperor, not as a "divine" supreme ruler surrounded by a mystical halo, untouchable, separated from ordinary Japanese by a system of taboos that ensured "worship at a respectful distance," as it had been before 1945, but as a "humble constitutional monarch close to the people. The main thrust of the revival of Tennoism in the early postwar years was a movement to restore Shintoism to the status of state religion. Since Shintoism has always emphasized the ritual side rather than the dogma, the preservation of many Shinto rituals after the defeat in the war, which, as we have seen, served to spread the cult of the emperor and militaristic chauvinistic sentiments among the masses, was regarded by Shintoists as the most important guarantee of successful activities to revitalize the political role of Shintoism. In this connection, since the emperor, who formally acted as a private person, actually continued to perform rites as the high priest of the national religion of Japan, and after his renunciation of his "divine" origin, there was still a basis for honoring the emperor as the guardian of traditional spiritual culture, which allowed the constitutional monarch of Japan to retain an implicitly important place in the system of nationalist symbols.

Thus, by the mid-1960s, a tendency to strengthen the power of the "symbolic imperial system" had emerged, and right-wing, reactionary forces began to propose turning the emperor into an actual head of state. However, the "non-political" nature of the emperor's activity as a symbol of the unity of the nation was often emphasized in words. Common to the speeches of many LDP politicians was the assertion that traditionally the emperor was not the holder of real political power, but was "the center of the unity of the nation" as the guardian of traditional morality. And it is due to this feature of the institution of imperial power that it not only "harmoniously combines" with the principle of popular sovereignty, but can even contribute to the "mutual prosperity" of the monarchical power and the power of the people [6, p. 205-206].

The Japanese authorities are building a new national idea of state nationalism on the basis of Tennoism. That is, a political course of uniting the people of the country to achieve high results in all areas of state development. By state nationalism in Japan (teikokusugi or kokkasugi) we understand historically specific state ideology and the practice of its application by the authorities of the country for political purposes. Japanese nationalism is a special ideological construct long ago created by the ruling elites in order to meet the internal and external needs of the nation and its specific interests. And in this respect, the nature of Japanese nationalism can be understood and explained both from the perspective of the theory of perennialism, which considers the development of a nation from the point of view of "long duree". That is, the long-term and continuous in time component of its historical development, and from the positions of modernists who consider the development of the nation and types of nationalism as a result of their recent modernization. [4,231c]. According to modernist theory, it is in the period of modernization that the state and ruling elites mobilize and unite the nation with the help of a new nationalist ideology, usually more aggressive and offensive than the previous one. And this is done to make it easier to fit in and hold on to the new system of international relations, the stable stay in which, as a rule, is associated with new challenges and threats to the survival of the nation

It seems to us that this approach to understanding modern Japanese state nationalism allows us to highlight its specific feature, which indicates that it is developing not so much as an independent modern ideology, such as, for example, liberalism, conservatism, socialism, with its own set of ideas and system of values, but only as a skillful substitution of them, which is deliberately introduced by the state into mass public consciousness through the spread of emotional feelings, patriotism, and the necessity to develop the nationalist ideology.

In other words, post-Cold War Japanese state nationalism is a state ideology that is highly demanded by the government and society for the purposes of the nation's survival in the twenty-first century. This ideology, like any other state ideology, can be seen as progressive or reactionary, reflecting left-wing or right-wing political views and beliefs. But in its absence or weakness, Japan would be doomed to lose the economic and political position of a world power it gained in the second half of the 20th century. In defining nationalism in general, Max Weber once correctly, in our opinion, emphasized that nationalism is an ideology created by the authorities for society and offering it its "story" about the "good" nation, its relations with the state and with other countries. The Japanese authorities, activating today the ideology of state nationalism, "tell" the society from positive positions about the special uniqueness of the Japanese nation, about its huge creative potential, as well as about the tasks of the authorities to preserve and improve it. At the same time, the ruling elite of Japan every time carefully "hints" to the nation that its survival in the hostile world environment in the 21st century is possible only by uniting the collective efforts of all Japanese "under the leadership of the emperor and the state" to protect the independence and sovereignty of the country and fulfill the priority tasks of national development.

Japanese state nationalism at the present stage of its development is a complex of ideological views and political practice of the Japanese authorities, in which the central place is given to the manipulation of the mass consciousness of the Japanese people on behalf of the nation and for its benefit. At the same time, the authorities quite effectively indoctrinate Japanese people with the ideas of their national superiority over other nations and consolidate the nation-state on this basis. It is noteworthy that nationalism and nationalist ideology in Japan did not decline by the beginning of the XXI century, contrary to the downward trajectory of this phenomenon predicted by a number of theorists (for example, Anthony Smith), but, on the contrary, are gaining momentum. This is due, in our opinion, to the decisive circumstance that the Japanese authorities, even in the early 21st century, see their historical purpose in preventing the entry into Japanese society of new global forces with ideologies alien to the Japanese, which can only destroy the unity of the nation and its "uniqueness."[4, 244c.] Nationalism in Japan today remains a unifying, protective force. Perhaps it will remain so in the future. And this is only due to the fact that nationalism as a state ideology in Japan has always found support from the overwhelming part of society, it is inseparable from the existence and survival of the Japanese nation and the Japanese state. The authorities subtly manipulate national feelings, myths, and traditional Japanese culture. They are ready at any moment to correct emerging deviations in the national ideology and direct it in the right direction. The authorities of modern Japan are interested in making every effort to "awaken dormant nationalism in society", based on the understanding that this is "nationalism healthy for the nation".

At the turn of the XX-XXI centuries, we are witnessing a renaissance of Japanese nationalism, when, after the Cold War, the period of American occupation essentially ended for Japan and the U.S. let it "free float" in the new chaotic and unstable system of international relations of the multipolar world, which replaced the relatively stable bipolar world order. The current ruling elite of Japan (no matter which political party is in power in Japan today - conservatives or democrats) is confident in its ability to mobilize traditional Japanese nationalism. The Japanese authorities have proved that they are capable of resuscitating (after the first defeat of the nation in the history of the state in World War II) a unique phenomenon - the Japanese nation-state in spite of serious efforts of the USA to destroy it from the root. This was possible only thanks to the use of traditional nationalism as the main "building material". As a result, the Japanese authorities ensured the progressive development of the nation-state, balanced and versatile economic growth, high living standards of the bulk of the population, and openness of channels of communication and self-expression of the Japanese people. Through the ideology of nationalism in Japan, an organized, efficient and responsive population and, importantly, a mature, morally upright, clean and flexible political elite were nurtured. Relying on the ideology of nationalism, the Japanese authorities learned to reproduce a generally successful model of national development, which ensured national sovereignty and independence of the nation. The nation-state in Japan has proven the possibility of stable existence of a nation with a homogeneous national identity that can serve as a model of healthy national development for many countries in the world.[3, p 2] The Japanese authorities will continue to make consistent efforts to strengthen the "spirit of the nation," without, of course, resorting to the propaganda of racism in the form of "skull shape, blood purity or genes," or calling society to violence or a culture of cruelty, as is often done by the authorities of other states. Japanese ruling circles, unlike the nationalist practices of many countries, do not intend in their propaganda of the ideology of nationalism to create a sense of disgust in society. On the contrary, they aim at maintaining the Japanese people's belief in the superiority of the Japanese nation and state, and at spreading nationalist ideology, especially among Japanese youth. The authorities of the country will subtly process the consciousness of future generations of Japanese, working "for the long term". The Japanese authorities manage to do this effectively, even though the Japanese travel a lot around the world, live on their territory together with migrants from other countries, exist in a world of wide transnational and globalized markets, global consumerism and mass communications.

Thus, today we can talk about the restoration of an ideology serving the interests of nationalist forces in the Japanese political reality. And the most important thing here is that the ultimate goal of this activity is to influence the minds of the younger generation of Japanese in the direction desired by the authorities. Japanese nationalists today work in the legislative and executive branches of government, schools and universities. They have already formed a network of organizations supporting nationalist ideology throughout the country. At the same time, Japanese nationalists do not work within elite structures, whose activities are not particularly visible on the surface, but go to the people, spreading nationalist ideology: they correct school textbooks and influence the mass consciousness of the Japanese through the media.

Nationalist ideas resonate and are understood in influential circles of Japanese society. The entire history of Japan is a history of interaction with other cultures. Such qualities of the Japanese as tolerance, ability to adapt, absorption of elements of other cultures became the prerequisites for rapid modernization of the country. Cultural interaction is a natural and inevitable process of civilizational development. However, due to the difference of cultures and value systems, any phenomenon adapted by another culture takes on a new appearance through a period of assimilation and reinterpretation. Throughout modern history, the Japanese identity was formed in the coordinate system defined by two poles - East and West, and gravitated alternately to one and the other pole. [4, c.48]

In order to determine what Japan has become today and what the Japanese themselves say about their nation, let us take some typical judgments about today's Japan related to national identity, which exist in the Japanese, but to a greater extent in the Western mass consciousness, and show that many of them are flattened and schematized stereotypes. Japan is a modern democratic society dominated by liberal values.

In 2008, the Institute of Mathematical Statistics conducted an opinion poll that asked for the first time whether Japan should be a society of free competition or one that supports the weak. The answer surprised the researchers. Only 22% were in favor of free competition and 73% were in favor of supporting the weak. [5,136c.] This once again proves the spirit of collectivism among the Japanese, they are sure that they will be able to move forward to a bright future only with mutual help and assistance. Then they will reach a common harmony, and will reduce the level of social distinction.

Institutionally, today's Japan is not strikingly different from contemporary Western standards. Post-war Japan has organically internalized the system of checks and balances and is accustomed to conducting elections according to Western democratic standards. The multiparty system functions largely according to well-studied canons. Japan, with some reservations, can serve as an example of well-functioning democratic mechanisms and, of course, in terms of institutional parameters, is a fully formed Western-style society.

However, significant differences are immediately apparent if we look at the specifics of the functioning of these institutions. Having borrowed the main elements of the modern democratic institutional system from the West, Japanese society has superimposed on them some traditional features of the national political culture. Western-type democratic institutions function on a distinctly different basis. For example, it is well known that important political decisions in Japan, as a rule, are made by the leaders of parliamentary factions, and only then stamped by voting in the parliament or the government. Naturally, behind-the-scenes maneuvering is also characteristic of Western societies, but in Japan the procedures of complex coordination and consensus-seeking are as if consecrated by tradition and play a fundamentally more important role than in the West.

The Japanese still value stability above the straightforwardness of democratic procedures and the omnipotence of the press, which can cause unnecessary turmoil and destroy the stability cherished.

The Japanese are now more indifferent to their country than they used to be. Many people remember the Japan of the 1960s and 1970s, swept by a wave of national pride, in a single impulse building its "economic miracle". It is known that in the late 1940s and early 190s, the Japanese massively limited personal consumption and directed part of their savings to the development of the country to overcome the consequences of the war. As we can see from Table 2 [6, c139], the feeling of love for one's country has been quite stable over the last 20 years, and mostly this indicator was above 50%. if we look back another 10 years, approximately the same picture. It is noteworthy that an upward trend is found in recent years, and in 2008 the index reaches its peak - 57%. The index reaches its peak of 57%. The same stability is demonstrated by this index for those who have little attachment to their country and for those who are indifferent. It can be concluded that the feeling of love for Japan is practically independent of crises and turns of political events.

A much more interesting picture emerges if we look at the distribution of answers by age categories (Table 3) [7, p. 139]. First of all, it is striking that at the age of 20-29 years old only 4.1% of respondents admit to a strong love for their country. In the category of 70-year-olds there are 41.2% of true patriots. That is 10 times more! Among those who do not feel any love for Japan at all, 20-year-olds are almost three times more numerous than 70-year-olds. It is in the age group from 20 to 39 that the greatest indifference to their country is observed. However, it should be clarified that some young people simply like to eupatize others with their cosmopolitanism. After 40 years of age, patriotic feelings begin to avalanche. This suggests that young people in Japan, due to their immature age and the influence of globalization, are indeed a group with a special attitude to patriotism.

Another major characteristic of Japanese society is hard work. "Theory about the Japanese" proclaim: labor for the inhabitants of the Land of the Rising Sun represents self-value, and income and success are by-products of self-forgetful labor. One of the socio-cultural stereotypes of traditional Japan is that man lives not because of himself, but because of his "neighbors" and the natural environment. Labor was considered almost the only way to repay "debts", and the Japanese owe everyone around them - parents, teachers, colleagues, friends, company, nation, the whole world. Hard work as a trait of national character continues to be a subject of respect. According to the Institute of Mathematical Statistics, hard work in 1958 was a priority value for 55% of respondents, and half a century later in 2008, 67% called it a strong point of the Japanese national character.[8, p 153].

The education of a child plays an important role in Japanese society. In the younger generation it is necessary to bring up all the worthy qualities of the Japanese people, to pass on all the spiritual wealth, culture, traditions, history, worldview, ideology - after all, this is the guarantor of a bright and stable future of the people. And it is not surprising that all the responsibility for the educational part falls on the shoulders of the mother. Usually a Japanese mother sits at home until the baby is three years old, after which he is given to a kindergarten. In Japan, there are also nurseries, but raising a young child in them is not encouraged. It is universally believed that children should be cared for by the mother. If a woman gives her child to a nursery and goes to work, her behavior is often seen as selfish. Such women are said to be insufficiently devoted to the family and put their personal interests first. And in Japanese morality, the social always prevails over the personal. But at the age of three, the child is sent to kindergarten. According to the Japanese, a child from early childhood should be able to behave in a team, to get acquainted with the spirit of collectivism. Groups in Japanese kindergartens are small: 6-8 people. And every six months their composition is re-formed. This is done in order to give kids more opportunities for socialization. If the child has not developed relationships in one group, it is quite possible that he will make friends in another. The caregivers are also constantly changing. This is done so that children do not get too used to them. Such attachments, the Japanese believe, give birth to the dependence of children on their tutors. What kind of classes are held in kindergarten? Children are taught to read, count, write, that is, prepare for school. If the child does not attend kindergarten, such preparation is done by mom or special "schools", which resemble Russian circles and studios for preschoolers. But the main task of a Japanese kindergarten is not educational, but educational: to teach the child to behave in a collective. In his future life he will have to be in a group all the time, and this skill will be necessary. Children are taught to analyze the conflicts that have arisen in games. In this case, you should try to avoid competition, because the victory of one can mean "loss of face" of the other. The most productive solution to conflicts, according to the Japanese, is compromise. Even in the ancient Constitution of Japan it was written down that the main dignity of a citizen is the ability to avoid contradictions. It is not customary to interfere in children's quarrels. It is believed that it prevents them from learning to live in a collective. An important place in the system of education is occupied by choral singing. To single out the soloist, according to Japanese ideas, is not pedagogical. And singing in chorus helps to cultivate a sense of unity with the collective. After singing it is the turn of sports games: relay races, salki, catch-up. It is interesting that educators, regardless of age, participate in these games equally with children. About once a month the whole kindergarten goes on a full day hike in the neighborhood. The places can be very different: the nearest mountain, zoo, botanical garden. In such hikes children not only learn something new, but also learn to be hardy, to endure hardships Much attention is paid to arts and crafts: drawing, applique, origami, oyachiro (weaving patterns from a thin rope stretched on the fingers). These activities perfectly develop fine motor skills, which are necessary for schoolchildren to write hieroglyphics. In Japan, children are not compared to each other. The teacher will never mark the best and scold the worst, will not tell parents that their child draws badly or best of all runs. It is not customary to single someone out. There is no competition even in sporting events - friendship or, in extreme cases, one of the teams wins. "Don't stand out" is one of the principles of Japanese life. But it does not always lead to positive results.

Thus, a new national idea helped post-war Japan to restore its state and find a strategic path for the country's development. The national idea was based on the ideology of Tennoism and state nationalism. The ideology of Tennoism was used in order not to lose one's self, reminding of the emperor, traditions, customs, religion of the Japanese people. The ideology of nationalism was used to unite the people, to make the people believe and realize their uniqueness, that together they are capable of many things. Japanese state nationalism after the Cold War is a state ideology that is highly demanded by the government and society for the purpose of survival of the nation in the XXI century. Japanese state nationalism at the present stage of its development is a complex of ideological views and political practice of the Japanese authorities, in which the central place is given to the manipulation of the mass consciousness of the Japanese on behalf of the nation and for its benefit.

At the same time, the authorities quite effectively indoctrinate Japanese people with the ideas of their national superiority over other nations and consolidate the nation-state on this basis. And the most important thing here is that the ultimate goal of this activity is to influence the minds of the younger generation of Japanese in the direction the authorities want. Japanese nationalists are now working in the legislative and executive branches of government, schools and universities. They have already formed a network of organizations supporting nationalist ideology throughout the country. At the same time, Japanese nationalists do not work within elite structures, whose activities are not particularly visible on the surface, but go to the people, spreading nationalist ideology: they correct school textbooks and influence the mass consciousness of the Japanese through the media.

2.2 Japan's modern political system

Japan is a democratic unitary state governed by the rule of law with a parliamentary monarchy as the form of government. The principles of governance are determined by the current Constitution (the supreme law of the land), which grants sovereign power to the people, guarantees fundamental human rights (respect for all people as individuals, equality of all people before the law, the right to elect and remove public officials, the right to peacefully petition for redress of grievances, the removal of public officials, the enactment, repeal or amendment of laws, decrees and regulations, freedom of thought and conscience, assembly and association, and the right to freedom of association, assembly and association.

The Constitution specifically stipulates the status of the emperor, who is a symbol of the state and the unity of the people, but is not vested with powers related to the exercise of state power, and defines the areas of competence of Parliament, the Cabinet of Ministers and local self-government bodies.

Emperor of Japan

The origin of the Japanese imperial house is shrouded in oddities, legends and prejudices. Here is at least one amazing fact: the ruling dynasty has not been interrupted for at least one and a half thousand years. Another fact: unlike European monarchs, unlike all other Japanese families, houses, clans and clans, the imperial house has no surname - a thing unthinkable for Europe. The position of the ruling house in Japan was so peculiar and strong that it simply did not need any surname.

The figure of the Japanese "emperor" was sacred. But it was a different kind of sacredness from Europe. It was a kind of inviolability - in the sense that the Japanese emperor did not become the subject of pictorial or verbal representation, or did so to a minimal degree. The Japanese emperor resembles a Shinto deity, who is generally never depicted either. With the exception of ancient mythological and chronicle vaults, we have extremely little "living" evidence to assist us in portraying Japanese rulers.

In ancient times, the ruler of Yamato (Japan) was simply called "great lord" (ookimi). If there were lords (kimi), there was a great lord among them. That is, the ruler was "merely" the first among equals. However, as the territory of the state expanded and the authority of the ruling family increased, a symbolic justification of this position was increasingly required.

The Japanese rulers of ancient times had at least three names: child, adult, and posthumous. From the ideological point of view, the most important was the multicomponent posthumous name, which best reflected what the ruling elite wanted to instill in itself, and at the same time in everyone else. The posthumous name of Emperor Temmu includes the following word combination, which is directly related to Chinese political thought: Heavenly Sage from Oki (Oki no Mahito), - one of the three sacred Taoist mountains, where immortal sages dwelt. The earthly emperor was thus likened to a heavenly divine lord. That is why the imperial edicts so often used the expression "kamunagara" - "Being a deity". The ruler's throne room was called either the "purple palace" (purple being the most sacred color) or the "Hall of the Great Limit". The concept of the Great Limit expressed the idea of the ultimate state of being, from which the feminine and masculine beginnings, and then the whole being, are born by successive doubling.

The attributes of imperial power in Japan are a sword, a mirror, and a jasper seal. Iron swords and bronze mirrors are found in abundance during excavations of ancient burial mounds, i.e. they were already believed to have sacred power. The seal throughout the Far East is an attribute of certain powers. Earlier, before the onset of comprehensive Chinese influence, the role of the seal was performed by the magatama - a plate of semi-precious stone, made in the shape of a comma. All three regalia are handed down from generation to generation when a new emperor ascends the throne.

The coat of arms of the Imperial House is a sixteen-petaled chrysanthemum. It is often depicted as a modern state symbol - for example, on foreign passports. In Japanese culture, the chrysanthemum was considered a sign of longevity, due to the chrysanthemum's known resistance to cold weather. Legend reports that, near a river on a rock grew a lot of chrysanthemums. Dew from the flowers rolled into the water, and those people who drank water from the river, were distinguished by excellent health and longevity. Hence the belief that wine infused with chrysanthemum petals extends life up to 8,000 years.

The ruling family of Japan considered itself a descendant of the main deity of the Shinto pantheon, Amaterasu. The dominant position of this family was originally conditioned by kinship with the deity of the sun. It was blood kinship that provided the emperor and his descendants with the throne, all other considerations played no role. None of the possible rivals of the imperial family could claim that, in case of overthrow of the ruling house, someone would recognize him as the legitimate sovereign. Therefore, attempts to overthrow the emperor are also almost non-existent in Japanese history.

Up until the Meiji Renewal, the order of succession in Japan was not defined. At present, the throne is passed only through the direct male line. Until then, any representative of the ruling family could theoretically become emperor or empress.

Therefore, the childlessness of the emperor or the absence of sons in his offspring did not lead to the interruption of the dynasty, as it happened in European and Russian history. Nevertheless, it was still considered preferable for direct male heirs of the ruling tenno to take the throne.

With very few exceptions, the Japanese emperor never possessed the full range of commanding powers that his European and Russian monarchical counterparts possessed. Thus, the appearance of the Japanese emperor in the theater of war as supreme commander-in-chief looks absolutely impossible. The tenno does not leave the confines of the capital, does not travel either within the country or, even more so, abroad, since the main function of the tenno is to stay in the sacral center, i.e. in the palace. The emperor participates in the rituals as the chief priest of Shinto, he is worshipped as a living deity, but he is obliged to maintain ritual purity and therefore does not touch worldly affairs. The very fact that he is on the throne is the most reliable guarantee that things are going well in the country. The other most important function of the emperor is the speech function, because it was in his name that decrees were proclaimed. Another function of the emperor was time management, a task that in ancient societies was usually performed by priests. The calendars drawn up at the end of the year were distributed to all institutions and provinces on behalf of the ruler. Thus, it was the emperor who was the "master" of the future time and regulated its course. The emperor also had the right to rename the motto before the expiration of his term of office. No purely ecclesiastical calendars existed in the country. The emperor exercised control over the past time with the help of annals - it was at his command that they were compiled by officials, not by monarchs, as was the custom in Russia.

The structure of Japanese power over the last thousand and fifteen hundred years has been such that the real commanding power has almost always been vested not in the emperor himself, but in another person or institution, making the tenno fundamentally invulnerable to any criticism that might be directed at him. In antiquity it was the head of the family. In medieval times it was the military rulers, the shoguns, who were formally appointed by sovereign decree. In modern times, the function of governing the country was assumed by the parliament and the government.

The current status of the emperor, which the post-World War II constitution defines as a symbol of the unity of the nation, fits well with historical realities. All sociological surveys show that there are extremely few people who would be in favor of abolishing the institution of tenno.

Constitution of Japan 1947.

Preparation and adoption of the constitution. An initial draft of Japan's constitution was prepared by the Japanese government with the help of a group of advisors in 1946, shortly after Japan's defeat in World War II. It retained many of the provisions of the country's first, conservative constitution of 1889, which enshrined the emperor's enormous power and a militaristic bureaucratic system. The draft was submitted to the parliament, but it provoked a negative reaction from the Japanese public and the Far Eastern Commission established by the victorious countries. As a result, the draft was actually withdrawn and, at the insistence of the Far Eastern Commission, the government submitted to the Diet a new text, developed, in essence, at the headquarters of the American occupation troops. In preparing the second draft, some principles of Anglo-Saxon law, new aspects of the development of constitutional law in the world (for example, provisions on the social and economic rights of citizens), as well as a private draft constitution prepared by a group of Japanese authors on the basis of the Weimar Constitution of Germany in 1919 were used.

The second draft, overcoming the resistance of reactionary circles, was adopted by Parliament in the fall of 1946 and, having received the approval of the Far Eastern Commission, entered into force on May 3, 1947.

The main provisions of the constitution. The Constitution of Japan is small in length:

it consists of 103 short articles. Unlike the 1889 Constitution, it proclaims the principle of popular sovereignty. The emperor is deprived of power and remains only a symbol of the nation. Parliament was proclaimed the supreme organ of the state and the only legislative body. The constitution speaks of some common values of mankind, the need to follow universal principles of political morality, that no state should proceed only from its own interests and ignore the interests of others.

Japan's Constitution took into account the sad experience of the military defeat of the country by the United States using nuclear weapons: the Constitution contains principled anti-war provisions. It states that the Japanese people are determined to prevent the horrors of a new war resulting from governmental action. The constitution has a special chapter on "renunciation of war" containing one article (Art. 9), which Japanese reactionary circles have repeatedly but unsuccessfully tried to revise. It stipulates that the Japanese people forever renounce war as a sovereign right of the nation, as well as the threat or use of force as a means of settling international disputes. To this end, the constitution states, no land, naval, or air force, or other means of warfare, shall ever be established. Japan has a Defense Corps, essentially the country's armed forces, but it spends approximately 1% of the national budget on its maintenance. The constitutional provision that the government of the country shall consist only of civilians is also aimed against the revival of militarism.

The Japanese Constitution contains a broad list of rights and freedoms of citizens. Along with traditional personal rights, provisions on the abolition of privileged estates (principalities, peerages, etc.), a list of traditional political rights (freedom of speech,' association, etc.), the constitution enshrines some social and economic rights (labor, education, etc.).

The Constitution establishes the system of state organs and their relations characteristic of a constitutional monarchy. In terms of territorial and political structure, Japan is a unitary state with wide local autonomy of administrative-territorial units (in practice, this autonomy is narrower than according to the law). The country has a democratic state regime.

Amending the constitution. The Constitution provides for a rather strict procedure for its amendment. It is possible only on the initiative of the Parliament, and amendments require the consent of 2/3 of the total number of members of each of its two chambers. After that, the amendments must be submitted for approval by referendum or must be reconsidered and approved by a new parliament, for which special parliamentary elections may be held. Once one of these procedures is completed, the constitutional amendment is considered to have taken place. Japan's constitution has not been amended since 1947.

Constitutional control. The final decision on the unconstitutionality of a normative act (law, decree, administrative act) in Japan, as in the United States, is made by the Supreme Court. However, unlike in the USA, the issue of constitutionality is discussed and decided outside the consideration of a criminal or civil case. In Japan, a special suit on the unconstitutionality of an act is filed in the court of first instance and the case can be brought to the Supreme Court by the hierarchy. This court in Japan is conservative and very rarely recognizes regulations as unconstitutional: only one provision of a law has been recognized as unconstitutional in the entire period of its operation.

The legal position of the Emperor of Japan.

Theoretically, in accordance with the concept of separation of powers, the branch of executive power may include the emperor (head of state) and the government (Cabinet of Ministers), but in reality only the government has power. The Constitution stipulates that executive power is exercised by the Cabinet of Ministers.

Emperor. Japan has a Salic system of succession to the throne: the throne is passed to the eldest son, women cannot inherit the throne. The reign of each emperor is proclaimed a special era, from the date of ascension to the throne of the new emperor the official chronology is carried out (since 1989 - the era of Emperor Akihito). In accordance with the Imperial House Law of 1947, the order of succession is ensured by the Imperial House Council, which consists of two members of the imperial family, the prime minister, the presidents and vice-presidents of the chambers, and one member of the Supreme Court.

Traditionally, the life of the emperor, who used to be considered a "son of heaven" of divine origin (his divine origin was first denied by Emperor Hirohito in 1946), and his family was surrounded by mystery, with government officials and the imperial court shielding him from contact with ordinary people. But in recent years, the openness of the life of the emperor and his family has increased (Emperor Akihito's wife comes from a simple family).

The emperor is an inviolable person and does not bear any responsibility - civil, criminal, administrative. The government and ministers are responsible for his actions. The emperor and members of his family receive funds from the state budget for their needs, but the amount of these funds is small. The daily affairs of the emperor and his family are handled by the Imperial Court Department, which is attached to the Prime Minister's Office. Any property may be transferred to members of the imperial family and any gifts received by them only with the permission of Parliament.

Both constitutionally and actually, the emperor has no personal power. In contrast to the former order, he is only a symbol of the unity of the state and the unity of the people, a person who owes his position to the people (Article 1 of the Constitution). The emperor has no powers of state power; all his actions connected with state affairs are carried out only with the advice and consent of the Cabinet of Ministers. The emperor performs mainly ceremonial functions of foreign policy, attends official celebrations and national holidays, and signs documents submitted to him by the prime minister.

By decision of the Cabinet, the Emperor exercises the following functions:

promulgates constitutional amendments, laws, publishes government decrees, international treaties, summons Parliament to session and dissolves the lower house, sets the date for parliamentary elections, certifies the appointments and resignations of ministers and certain other senior officials, confirms the credentials of ambassadors and envoys, receives foreign ambassadors and their credentials, confirms amnesties, grants awards and honors. He appoints the Prime Minister by decision of Parliament and, on the latter's nomination, the members of the Cabinet and the Chief Justice of the Supreme Court.

Most of these powers are traditionally reserved for the head of state, although the Japanese constitution does not characterize the emperor as the head of state. He is legally powerless, does not engage in state policy, but traditionally influences the political and ideological life of the country.

Modern society today is increasingly interested in the Imperial House. The unique preservation of traditions, faith and worship of the Emperor, national consciousness, the attitude of the Japanese people to their homeland - arouses interest not only among scholars, politicians, but also among ordinary lovers of all things Japanese. The most common questions include: How does the nation behave today? Do they sincerely believe or is it a formality for them? All public opinion questions show that there is no anti-monarchical sentiment. There are sharply pro-monarchy sentiments (far-right), but they are very few. Culture does not pose such a question: do we need an emperor or not? He is there and that's it. It is a given, and people do not think about it. What about the tax system? After all, it turns out that the people actually support the emperor, paying taxes for his maintenance. And in this regard, there are no questions. It's all in the order of things. Every Japanese considers it his duty to serve the emperor. In the past, he used to give part of his crops to the treasury of the Imperial House; today he pays taxes.

The next question of interest is what kind of education does the future emperor receive? Where does he receive his primary education, does he then go to university? School education - at home. Further - to the university in Japan. The question remains relevant - is the emperor accessible to ordinary people? Traditionally, the emperor could not be seen. For a long time there was a ban on seeing him. The ban is quite strong. And it comes from the deepest antiquity. Even legends have been preserved which say: "So-and-so became king and since then no one has seen him". The Chinese in the 6th century witnessed the Japanese saying that their ruler sleeps during the day and is awake at night. Darkness in traditional culture is a companion to invisibility. Nowadays, of course, things are not so strict. The emperor appears on the television screen quite a lot. But still his voice can be heard quite rarely. The ban on mere mortals being able to hear him speak was lifted only after the war, when Emperor Shōwa addressed the nation by radio. It was then that people heard his voice for the first time. Before that, almost no one had heard the Emperor's voice. [34, c.3]

Parliament of Japan, its structure. Methods of adopting laws.

According to the constitution, the only legislative body in Japan is the Diet.

Structure of the Parliament. The Japanese parliament consists of two chambers, the House of Representatives (lower) and the House of Councillors (upper), which are elected by the above methods. The House of Representatives is elected for a 4-year term of 500 members (511 until 1996), the House of Councillors consists of 252 councillors elected for a 6-year term, but with half of them rotating every three years. The House of Representatives can be dissolved early by an act of the emperor at the request of the government (Cabinet of Ministers), the upper house is not subject to dissolution.

MPs and advisers have a free mandate and enjoy limited parliamentary immunity: they may not be arrested during a session, and if arrested before the session, they must be released for the duration of the session on the request of the relevant chamber. However, an MP may be expelled at any time from any chamber by a resolution of the majority of the members of the chamber present (provided a quorum is present). MPs and Councillors enjoy indemnity, are professional parliamentarians and receive remuneration from the public treasury.

The internal structure of the chambers is similar; it is determined by the Law on Parliament and the rules of procedure of the chambers. Each chamber elects a chairman, a vice-chairman, a temporary chairman (who presides over sessions when the first two officials are unable to perform their duties), chairmen of standing committees (commissions) and a general secretary of the chamber (the latter is not elected from among the deputies and deals with organizational issues) for the entire term of office. Party factions are established in the chambers, which play a decisive role in the allocation of leadership positions in the chambers and other posts, as well as in the allocation of deputies to standing committees. There are 18 permanent specialized commissions in the House of Representatives and 16 in the Chamber of Councillors. Their profile usually corresponds to different spheres of public life and administration (commissions on foreign affairs, agriculture, etc.); in Japan they are closely connected with the work of the relevant ministries, with the bureaucracy, although they have the right to control the work of the ministries. Each parliamentarian is obliged to be a member of one or two commissions. The chairman of the commission is elected from the members of the party faction with the largest representation in the commission, but in practice this is decided in advance during the division of the chairmanship during negotiations between faction leaders.

Commissions hold two types of meetings: working and general. The former deal with the most important issues and are usually attended by the Minister, and sometimes by the Prime Minister or other high-ranking official. General meetings deal with less important issues and are more often attended by parliamentary secretaries (deputy ministers representing the minister in parliament). As in other countries, commissions in Japan play a decisive role in the consideration of bills, and their fate is usually predetermined by the decision of the commission.

Each chamber has legislative bureaus - a special internal body that assists deputies in their work on bills and controls the passage of government bills. The bureaus have their own apparatus, with several offices staffed by professional civil servants. This form again ensures close links between the parliament and Japan's extensive bureaucracy.

The chambers have secretariats made up of non-parliamentarians, headed by the general secretary of the chamber. There are various research, reference and administrative services for deputies and advisers, and a large library where more than 150 employees work on the preparation of various research and reference materials at the request of the deputy.

Powers of the parliament. The main task of the Japanese parliament, as well as parliaments of other democratic countries, is legislation, in particular, determining state revenues and expenditures - the state budget. The Constitution stipulates that the parliament is the only legislative body, the head of state (the emperor) does not participate in legislation and does not have the right to veto laws.

The House of Representatives plays a major role in the legislative process in Japan, as in many other countries, because in certain cases acts passed by it become laws without the consent of the upper house: the lower house overrides the veto of the upper house by passing a law by a second veto by a 2/3 majority, with the votes of those present (the quorum in Japan is 1/3 of the members) and not of the general membership of the house A state budget law can also be passed without the participation of the upper house if all avenues for agreement have been exhausted. The lower house has other advantages.

The vast majority of bills in Japan, as in other countries, come to the Diet from the government (20 deputies or 10 advisors can also introduce a bill), but in Japan this happens after a thorough bureaucratic process that continues during the Diet's deliberations. Laws are usually drafted in ministry departments, after which the draft is passed on to the ministry leadership, reaches the minister, goes to the Prime Minister's Office (it is equal in rank to the ministry), then to the Prime Minister, and only then, on behalf of the government, is it submitted to the Diet. But even after that, bills are not yet subject to consideration in plenary session, at least in the form of a first reading. They are dealt with in the legislative bureau of the chamber and in parallel, and often even afterwards, in the relevant standing committee. Here the draft also undergoes a lengthy procedure of study and coordination (often special subcommittees are created to study the draft), and only after the commission has taken a positive decision is it submitted to the plenary session, where it is usually discussed in two readings (general discussion and at the same time article-by-article discussion with the report of the standing committee, and then adoption as a whole).

The bill then goes to the upper house, which must approve or reject the lower house's decision within 60 days. If it fails to do either within this period, the bill is considered rejected. In case of rejection, the lower chamber may override the upper chamber's veto in the above manner, but may also request the establishment of a parity conciliation commission (10 members from each chamber), or a joint session of the chambers is held. If the commission fails to come up with a compromise option or this option is not adopted by the chambers, the law is considered adopted in the text of the lower chamber and is subject to publication. In a joint sitting of the chambers, the decision is taken by a majority vote of the total number of parliamentarians, and the lower house, due to its larger number, has the upper hand.

The budget bill, as in other parliaments, is first submitted to the lower house. The budget discussion takes place with the mandatory participation of the Prime Minister and all ministers. Members of the public, citizens can participate in the discussion of this draft. Every citizen can apply to participate in the budget debate, and the chairman of the budget committee of the parliament usually selects several people from among those who have applied to speak in the debate.

If the House of Councillors does not approve the budget decision adopted by the lower house of parliament (in this case, the upper house has 30 days instead of 60) and no agreement is reached at a joint session of the chambers, the budget law as amended by the lower house is considered adopted.

Voting in parliament on bills and other decisions can be done in various ways: by standing up (counting is done), by secret ballots (parliamentarians receive two ballots of white and blue color: the first means "for", the second - "against"), by roll-call voting (in this case, an MP attaches a card with his/her name to the ballot), by polling (the chairman asks if there are any objections, and if there are none, the decision is adopted; if there are objections, another form of voting is used). Voting and debates in the Japanese parliament are often quite heated, with MPs often getting into fights.

The adopted law is signed by the minister responsible for non-implementation and the prime minister and sent to the emperor for signature. The emperor must sign the law within 30 days and publish it. The law comes into force 20 days after publication.

Of the other supreme organs of the state, the Japanese parliament forms only the government (Cabinet): the head of state is for life, the Supreme Court is not formed by the parliament. Parliament (lower house) exercises control over the activities of the government through questions in plenary sessions, inviting ministers to meetings of standing committees, but the main form of control is interpellation, for which Japan has a simplified procedure. The right to submit an interpellation in writing belongs to each member of the Lower House (through the Speaker of the House). If the Speaker refuses to accept the appeal, the Deputy may appeal directly to the plenary. An oral or written reply to an interpellation must be given within 6 days, and a vote is taken on the results of the reply.

Parliamentary investigations can be conducted by any chamber, for which special commissions are established. In a number of cases, the activities of such commissions have even led to the resignation of prime ministers found guilty of financial mismanagement and bribery (and their subsequent conviction). A form of parliamentary oversight is also the general discussion of government policy at the beginning of each session, when the Prime Minister speaks on government policy, followed by the Ministers of Foreign Affairs and Finance, who speak about the policies of their departments.

Sessions and meetings of the Parliament. Regular sessions of Parliament are convened once a year. An extraordinary session may be convened at the request of a quarter of the total number of members of one of the chambers (the other chamber is then also obliged to convene) or the Cabinet of Ministers. During the dissolution of the lower house, the Cabinet may convene an emergency session of the House of Councillors, but measures adopted at such a session are considered provisional and become null and void unless approved by the lower house within 10 days of its first meeting.

For the meetings of the chambers a quorum is required - the presence of at least 1/3 of the members of parliament. Meetings of standing commissions are valid with the participation of 2/3 of their members.

The Government of Japan, its composition and procedure of formation.

Cabinet of Ministers. The Cabinet consists of the Prime Minister, Ministers (there are currently 12 of them) and Ministers of State (there are 8 of them), who are usually advisers to the Prime Minister (he may also give them separate managerial assignments and sometimes even entrusts them with the management of certain spheres of public life). Traditionally, certain State Ministers are in charge of separate units of the Prime Minister's Office. The Cabinet also includes the Minister of the Cabinet (a kind of manager of government affairs) and the head of the Legislative Bureau, the body through which all government bills are passed (they are prepared very meticulously in Japan).

According to the constitution, at least half of the ministers must be elected from among members of parliament (in practice, all ministers are usually recruited from parliamentarians) and lose their parliamentary mandate upon appointment as a minister. Ministers enjoy certain safeguards when they are prosecuted: the consent of the Prime Minister is required. Ministers in Japan are usually not professionals; they are party politicians. They are frequently replaced and do not delve deeply into the affairs of their ministries. The real heads of the ministry are the administrative heads of the ministry staff. The role of professional bureaucracy in government, as in parliament, is great.

The government is formed by both houses of parliament (in fact, the lower house), but is officially appointed by decree of the emperor. First, each house of parliament elects a candidate for prime minister (until 1993 this was the leader of the Liberal Democratic Party, now it is the leader of the ruling coalition). Since each chamber has the right to nominate a candidate for prime minister, there may be disagreements between them. In such disagreements, and if the upper house does not nominate a candidate within 10 days of the beginning of the parliamentary session, the lower house's decision on the prime minister's candidacy is considered the parliament's decision. Normally, the upper house does not nominate a candidate other than the lower house, as it is useless. The elected Prime Minister considers nominations for ministerial posts submitted to him by the various factions of Parliament. In allocating these posts, determining their number, the "weight" of the ministries, the influence of the various factions is strictly taken into account. All members of the Cabinet are approved by decree of the Emperor. They must be civilians.

According to the constitution, the Cabinet performs the general functions of governance, including the duty to faithfully implement the constitution and laws and conduct the affairs of state. The Cabinet directs foreign policy, concludes international treaties (requiring prior or subsequent parliamentary approval depending on their nature), directs the civil service, submits the draft state budget to parliament, issues decrees to implement the constitution and laws (decrees may also include criminal penalties, but only on the basis of powers delegated by law). The Cabinet decides on amnesties, pardons and suspensions of sentences, and reinstatement of rights (the latter power was mainly related to the decision on the responsibility of various persons in connection with the events of the Second World War). Cabinet decrees are signed by the Prime Minister and the relevant Minister.

The Prime Minister holds a decisive position in the Cabinet, like the Chancellor in Germany. He actually appoints and removes members of the Cabinet, ensures the unity of its actions, and regulates disagreements between its members.

Cabinet meetings are governed by custom, they are closed to the public, and decisions are made by unanimous or consensus (no objectors, though not in favor) rather than by vote.

The Japanese government has established a wide network of advisory bodies that work closely with business organizations, trade unions, academia, members of parliament, and senior civil servants. They collect various information, conduct independent expertise of proposed and adopted decisions, and exercise a certain control over the activities of the bureaucratic apparatus.

Thus, today Japan is a dynamically developing country, and this is largely due to the natural industriousness and entrepreneurial spirit of the Japanese people. Striving for everything new and progressive, readiness to adopt and improve the latest world achievements - this quality of the Japanese people has long been a remarkable national tradition. Modern Japan demonstrates to the world a unique experience of forming an original political system. It is a country that immensely cherishes the traditions of its ancestors, possesses adequate, moderate conservatism and at the same time positively evaluates the existing experience of state-legal construction accumulated by the modern world. The ideology of Tennoism preserves the national color, traditions and customs. At the same time, it helps the country, in the current period of globalization, to absorb everything Western, new, and learn to adapt in the country, so that the Japanese handwriting is preserved.

Conclusion

State ideology is formed as a means of self-preservation of peoples, as a stimulus for development, as a spiritual and moral basis for the unity of individuals in the nation. The formation of state ideology coincided with the interests, attitudes, traditions, historically formed, particularly in Japan. In other words, the state ideology derived from the way of life of people and corresponded to their understanding of the world order. Over the course of more than a thousand years of history, the ideology of the institution of monarchical power has undergone a complex path of evolution - from the cult of the "sacred emperor" through a marked weakening of its influence on the spiritual life of society in the period of medieval feuds to its gradual revival in modern times as the central idea of national consciousness. During this time, "cross-cutting" ideas related to the ideas about the role of the institution of imperial power in the life of society were formed; they began to have a direct influence on the national psychology, including mass political consciousness. For a long period of the Middle Ages, the social significance of the institution of imperial power was determined, first of all, by the religious prestige of the tenno as the supreme clergyman of Shinto rites, led to the establishment of a tradition in political culture, when the nominal head of the hierarchy had no real power; he was perceived as a spiritual charismatic force exercising power through moral duty, and the actual supreme power (shoguns) was based on an extensive administrative apparatus of coercion. The institution of imperial power began to serve to legitimize the power of real rulers, while the basis for the preservation of sacral imperial power in medieval Japan was the stability of the traditional social structure. This did not mean that the political system did not change, of course, it changed and became more complex, but there was an evolutionary process of transformation of traditions, which is generally characteristic of the development of Japanese culture. New elements were always only added to the old structure, but never destroyed it. Gradually the new elements, which were modified as they adapted to the old structure, caused the restructuring of the whole system. The basis of state ideology is the recognition of the leading role of the state in the life of society, both in the narrow sense of the term "state", as a strong central authority, and in the broader sense, as a powerful organism, naturally integrating into its the composition of each individual. The existence of a state ideology is inextricably linked to religion. In the case of Japan, three religions. Shinto, Buddhism and Confucianism have left their indispensable contribution to the spiritual and moral consciousness of the Japanese people. As a spiritual component of people's life, state ideology necessarily contains certain moral, ethical attitudes that coincide with the moral attitudes of the main mass of people, although in some period of society's development state ideology can be imposed by force. In addition, the state ideology contains the principles and ideas of economic organization of society, the essence of which in the most general form can be expressed as follows: enriching the state, you enrich yourself. The state in the system of ideological values acts as an inevitable condition for the stability of the development of the economy and society as a whole.

Almost 70 years have passed since the surrender of militaristic Japan. The country's social and economic outlook has changed dramatically. But even today, the institution of imperial power is an organic element of Japanese reality. Tennoist ideology in its improved version is used to justify such socio-mythological complexes as "the enterprise is one family", "a man devoted to the company", "collectivism in the Japanese way", and other elements of paternalism. The basis for the formation of a unified national psychotype is still the original, ancient traditions of political culture in the form of an appeal to the ideological possibilities of the "symbolic imperial system" for the consolidation of the nation. But unlike in the pre-war period, the "symbolic" status of the emperor allows him to serve more fruitfully as the guardian of the traditional values of life of the Japanese image. In connection with the economic success of Japan and the aspiration of its leaders to turn the country into a world power, there was a growth of nationalist sentiments among the broadest masses of the population, which allowed the ruling class to resort to the development and propaganda of the official doctrine of nationalism (including, to a large extent, elements of tennoism). It should be emphasized, however, that this doctrine is not of an aggressive, expansionist nature. The "new" nationalist ideals, adjusted according to the dictates of the time, although outwardly secular in appearance, are still largely based on the cultural and religious notions of pre-war Tennoism. The institution of imperial power still has a halo of "sanctity" in the eyes of certain segments of the population. In other words, mass consciousness in contemporary Japan remains largely susceptible to the mythological symbolism of the imperial cult. The emperor fulfills the function of a passive spiritual-psychological symbol, the guardian of the nation's moral and religious values. The intensification of government initiatives to promote nationalist attitudes since the early 1980s is once again accompanied by the use of the mobilizing power of Shinto ritual with its mysticism orientation to cultivate a sense of unique ethnicity among the Japanese. These rituals are still designed to ensure the unconscious perception of nationalist stereotypes. Japanese culture, according to the modern ideologues of Tennoism, is interpreted as a suprapersonal spirit, and the guardian of this spirit is the emperor as the spiritual head of the nation. In the context of the modification of religion, the unanimous moral solidarity of the society should be ensured on the basis not so much of religious experience as of aesthetic experience, pursuing the same goal of developing a sense of community among the Japanese. The culture of Japan, of which the emperor is proclaimed the guardian, serves as the foundation for the revitalization of a sense of comradeship and community. Today we are witnessing the creation of a refined, "cultural" version of Japan's modern state myth.

On the example of the Japanese experience of state development, one comes to the conclusion that ideology in the state has a special place, that it is ideology that helps the country to unite to achieve common goals, and no factor from outside can destabilize this system. State ideology is especially important in Kazakhstan due to its historical development, the Soviet past, and the multi-ethnic composition of the people.

The first practical step towards the formation of a state ideology could be the development of a draft law "On the State". It could lay the legal foundations for: 1) the goals of the existence of the state; the interaction between the state, the people and the individual; 2) approve such moral system-forming values as: protection of the honor and dignity of the Republic; protection of the honor and dignity of the citizen of the Republic; on the symbols of the state and responsibility for abuse of them. It is necessary to prepare draft laws that would lay down the legal foundations for the formation of patriotism, the responsibility of the citizen to the State and the State to society, the responsibility for the upbringing of a worthy citizen of the country, the protection and encouragement of talented people of the country. And to all this we need a wide propaganda, which will unite the ideas of the people into a single whole, and will help the country, in the age of high competition and globalization, to resist and develop further towards a bright future.

LIST OF REFERENCES USED:

1.Ozhegova S.I. and Shvedova N.Y. Explanatory Dictionary of the Russian language.- M.: Izdvo "ITI Tekhnologii", 2006.-941s.

1.1 Remin V.N. Political system of modern Japanese society. - M.: Izd-wo Nauka, 1992. - 216c.

3 Bugaeva D.P. Japanese publicists of the end of the XIX century. Moscow: 1978.

4 Peoples and Religions of the World: Encyclopedia / Ed. by V.A.Tishkov. Editors: O.Y.Artemova, S.A.Arutyunov, A.N.Kozhanovsky, V.M.Makarevich (deputy editor-in-chief), V.A.Popov, P.I.Puchkov (deputy editor-in-chief), G.Y.Sitnyansky. - Moscow: Big Russian Encyclopedia, 1998 - 928 pp.

5 . Tosaka Jun Japanese ideology.- M.: izdvo "Progress", 1982.- 247c.

6 . Vasiliev L.S. History of religions of the East. Zen aesthetics. Confucianism in Japan. [Electronic document]. (http://www.alleng.ru/d/relig/relig007.htm). Checked 19.06.2012.

7 Svetlov G.E. The Way of the Gods (Shinto in the History of Japan).- M.: Mysl, 1985.

8 .Krupyanko M. I. and Areshidze L. G. Article - Japan: Ideology of State Nationalism

9 . Chugrov S.V. Japan in search of a new identity.- M.: publishing company "Oriental Literature" RAS, 2010.-311 pp.

10 History and culture of traditional Japan. - M.: publishing house "Natalis", 2010.-478s.

11 .Sila-Novitskaya T.G. The Cult of the Emperor in Japan.-M.: Main Editorial Office of Oriental Literature "Nauka", 1990.-206s.

12 . Makovsky V.D. Japan on the threshold of the XXI century.- M.: INION, 1989.

13 Makarov A.A. Political power in Japan: mechanism of functioning at the present stage. - M.: Nauka, 1988.

14 Shaimardanova N.J. The problem of constitutional revision.- Almaty//Kzakhstna-Spectrum, 2007/4(42)

15 Shaimardanova N.J. Democracy in Japanese.- Almaty/ZAnalytic, 2009/5(51)

16 E.V. Molodiakova, Japan: the change of political regime.- M.//Asia and Africa Today, 2010Z2

1. Eremin V.N. Political system of modern Japanese society.- M.: Nauka,1992.- 216 pp.

18. Pospelov B.V. Some aspects of ideological activity of the Japanese bourgeois state at the present stage. [Electronic document].

(http://ichiban.narod.ru/books/YAIKL/ikl02.html). Checked 06/19/2012.

19. Musikhin G.I. Discursive analysis of ideologies: opportunities and limitations. //Political Studies "Polis", 2011/5-175c.

20. Confucianism in Japan.- Peoples and Religions of the World.- Encyclopedia, M.: 1998.- 845c.

21. Spiritual Culture of the East.- History of Eastern Philosophy, textbook, M. 1988.- 175 pp.

22. Anisimtsev N. Transparency of administrative and public management: Japanese variant // Problems of theory and practice of management.- 2001, №6

23. Handbook on Japan's civil service statistical overview/- January, 1996.

24. Volgin N.A. Japanese experience in solving economic and socio-labor problems. - M.: Ekonomika, 1998.

25. Vasiliev A.A. The system of local self-government in Japan. //"MS NO", NO. 5-1995.

26. Reforming the system of public administration: foreign experience and

Kazakhstan. The most scientific edition.- Almaty: KISI under the President of RK, 2005.- 276p.

27. Hijikata Kadeuo. "Nihon bunka ron" to tennosei ideoorogi ("Theory of Japanese Culture" and Ideology of the Imperial System).- Tokyo, 1983.

28. Nihonjin no shiso to kodo (Thinking and Behavior of the Japanese).- Tokyo, 1973

29. Takahashi H. Your Majesty, let me address you.- Tokyo, 1988.350c.

30. Molodiakova E.V., "Unordinary" Democracy in Japan. // Japan: myths and reality.- M.: Izd.firm "Oriental Literature" RAS, 1989.- p.160178

31. Huntington S..The Clash of Civilization. // Polis.-1994.№1.-p.33-5

32. Meshcheryakova A.N. "The book of Japanese symbols". [Electronic document].

(http://www.japantravel.ru/rus/japan/147/document1762.htm).

Checked on 06/19/2015.

33. Hijikata Kadeuo. Theory of Japanese Culture" and the Ideology of the Imperial System.- Tokyo, 1983.

34. OKNOY TO JAPAN - Bulletin of the Society "Russia-Japan",# 41,16.11.2003 [Electronic document]. (http://ru-jp.orgru-jp@nm.ru). Checked 19.06.2015.

see Armstrong 1982; Seton-Watson 1965; Connor 1994; Horowitz 1985; Anderson 1991; Hobsbawn 1990). (see Heywood 2007 for more on this).

Printed by Books on Demand GmbH, Norderstedt / Germany